THE SILENT PATH—AN INTRODUCTION TO MEDITATION

THE SILENT PATH—
AN INTRODUCTION
TO MEDITATION

MICHAL J. EASTCOTT

SAMUEL WEISER INC.
New York

SAMUEL WEISER INC.
734 Broadway, New York 10003

First published 1969
This United States edition 1971

Printed in Great Britain
0–87728–063–0

CONTENTS

ILLUSTRATIONS

TECHNIQUES AND MEDITATION OUTLINES

FOREWORD

This book has been written because of the great interest in meditation today and the number of people asking for information on the fundamental questions that arise. It is offered, therefore, as a kind of everyman's guide to the ways and uses of meditation as a constructive part of living in our modern world, not an escape from it.

In all of us there is a mysterious activator urging us on up the long evolutionary way. Just as surely as this urge has brought us out of the primordial forests of long ago to our present concrete, steel and technological pinnacle, so will it not let us rest without exploring and laying claim to the dimensions of consciousness that lie ahead now.

It is to this eternal activator, divine principle—call it what we will—that this book is really directed, for it is this that first stirs and urges us to meditate, this that makes progress possible, and this that will in the end give the new dominions into our hands.

Another point should be made at the outset. The new-comer to meditation must not let himself be confused if he finds that it means different things to different people.

There are many paths which can be followed and each must find his own chosen way once he has equipped himself with the basic requirements. In this book no attempt has therefore been made to cover the whole field, because this extends through both the centuries and civilizations of human history and comprises specialized approaches, any one of which demands a lifetime, and more, for its full exploration. Rather, its aim is to put forward the reality and general direction of the hidden path that leads from world to world, like a causeway waiting to be found.

Yet it has also been written to give some encouragement, because this path is essentially a way we have to discover for ourselves, and it may sometimes seem a lonely one and its requirements an unrewarding discipline. But this is not so. Every time we attempt to reach beyond the immediate— with intelligence—we are extending ourselves towards our high potential, and this is our truest source of joy.

So when we start to meditate we launch upon a great enterprise. Also, we are not as alone in it as we may seem. On the silent path we have countless companions and belong to an honoured company, for not only has this way been trodden by the greatest of those who have walked on earth, but we are told the Buddha said of it:

It were better to live one single day in the pursuit of understanding and meditation than to live a hundred years in ignorance and unrestraint.

Though inland far we be,
  Our souls have sight of that immortal sea
Which brought us hither.

WORDSWORTH

I · THE SECRET PLACE

'We do not hear the sun rise,' wrote Paul Brunton, author of many books on meditation and the mysteries of the East. 'So, too, the greatest moment in a man's life comes quietly. In that stillness alone is born the knowledge of the Overself'. This gives the reason for the title of this book. The path of meditation can well be compared with the long stillness before daybreak. There is frequently nothing to mark it but a quietly increasing light. The gradual dawning of a new world in our consciousness comes silently. It is a secret, inner thing which we can never fully share with others—a silent path.

It must of necessity be so, even if we pursue it in the company of others, for it entails certain adjustments that we have to make in ourselves, it leads to recognitions that we only come by through our own endeavour, and it brings, eventually, knowledge—realization—that we only reach by personal experience. As the spider spins out of its own substance the thread it will proceed along, so we, through meditation, build our pathway out of our own consciousness. It must, therefore, be an inner, silent, secret path which we carve out for ourselves.

Yet there are many different kinds of silence, and meditation can be practised in the midst of sound. In fact it very often has to be today! We are compelled to slip it into whatever semi-quiet times we can find while life goes pulsing on around us. We are learning to accept that cloisters and hermits' caves are not to be found in modern society. The difficulty of finding any quiet today is one of the conditions of the advance of civilization; our growing powers place more demands on us. But this is evolution, and if we have to thread our way through countless impacts before we can make our approach to the inner places, this is the battleground of our present stage. Further, it underlies the fact that meditation is not simply an escape into day-dreams when the fancy moves us, but a specific use of our faculties to make an inner penetration. A quiet use, yes, but nevertheless a defined, deliberate and controlled use which demands both intention and effort.

Meditation is often mistakenly thought to be a negative procedure, but it requires many of the positive qualities that Christian was called upon to demonstrate in his more dramatic *Pilgrim's Progress*. These qualities are called for on a higher turn of the spiral, on inner, silent, unseen reaches, where they bring no glory or outward prestige. There are none to see our victories—whom we know of—and our long efforts, struggles and achievements seem known only to ourselves.

Yet our endeavour does not go unrewarded. The ramparts of the inner world are surrendered to us when we have proved ourselves. This is a matter of the law of vibration, of like being able to synchronize with like. We shall go into this later, but right from the start, it is wise to realize that meditation is not a passive form of devotion; it is a positive use of our highest capacities to bridge between the outer and inner worlds.

What makes us start with this undertaking? Perhaps the origin of the determination to meditate lies way back in the sense we all have—hidden in varying degrees—of an inner world or 'somewhere else', apart from everyday existence. It was with a great many of us persistently as children. We *knew* another world. We clothed it as our fancy led, were heroes there, achieved the impossible, possessed all attributes, rode as kings.

It was escape, of course, on the wings of imagination. But it was also more than that. It was a refraction of the sense of the reality of other dimensions. The magic world through the hole in the fence replaced dominions we were missing. Here we broke through all boundaries. It was 'holy'. And no matter how we clothed this secret world, it was where we withdrew to when we needed more than the world around us gave—or when that world, we considered, treated us badly. We told no one of it in case they spoilt it. We sensed it was lodged on ephemeral grounds. But in fact, it was built on something sounder than we had any idea of then—on a memory that still lingered and was not yet veiled entirely by louder and more tangible things.

Wordsworth still remembered it when he wrote 'Heaven lies about us in our infancy.' And—

Our birth is but a sleep and a forgetting:
The Soul that rises in us, our life's Star,
   Hath had elsewhere its setting,
   And cometh from afar.

Slowly we put on more and more of the world. As Wordsworth went on to say in *Intimations of Immortality*: 'Shades of the prison-house begin to close upon the growing boy.' The sense of the inner world inevitably slips away to a large extent, yet do we ever quite forget the special joy we dwelt there with as children, and have never quite recaptured since?

This recollection of an inner or secret or super world appears continually in the writings of all ages, quite apart

from religious teaching and the doctrines of the East, where
it is no strange thing and more or less generally accepted.
'All the poems of the poet who has entered into his poet-
hood are poems of homecoming,' Martin Heidegger wrote.
But according to Plato:

> All souls do not easily recall the things of the other
> world. Few only retain an adequate remembrance of
> them.

Plotinus put forward the same thought as Wordsworth in
these words:

> The soul . . . falling from on high, suffers captivity, is
> loaded with fetters, and employs the energies of sense.
> . . . Thus the soul, proceeding from the regions on high,
> becomes merged in the dark receptacle of body.

Goethe wrote in *Faust* of the soul in him which

> . . . seeks to rise in mighty throes
> to those ancestral meadows whence it came.

Thomas Vaughan drew a more attractive picture of our
sojourn on earth than most of the poets and philosophers:
'I look on this life as the progress of an essence royal; the
soul but quits her court to see the country.'

But however we may regard the contraposition of
the inner and outer spheres of life, most will agree with
Emerson:

> The Genius which according to the old belief stands at
> the door by which we enter, and gives us the lethe to
> drink, that we may tell no tales, mixes the cup too
> strongly, and we cannot shake off the lethargy now at
> noon day. Sleep lingers all our lifetime about our eyes.

Hence our efforts, like someone stirring in his sleep before he wakes, to penetrate the mists that hang between the two domains and to investigate all kinds of methods holding any promise of showing a way through.

The beautiful, the fanciful, the strange, the unknown, all awake some echo in our half-starved souls, and hungrily we respond, hoping we may find something to satisfy our unframed yearning, or even some clue to the source of this indefinable nostalgia. The storytellers and poets—and there are many—who have written in answer to this 'pull' to the unknown world are among the most famous and most widely read.

Eagerly men have feasted from the earliest times on the sagas, legends, folk tales and allegories that fed the imprisoned sense of infinity, and reiterated the promise of the Isles of the Hesperides and the Lands of Lyonnesse. Almost everyone has at some time found a special story that has fanned the spark deep in his heart into a glow that lasted, secretly, for most of his life-time. From Malory to de la Mare, and east and west wherever words have been written, we have, to paraphrase Thomas Hardy's lines in *The Oxen*, gone with them gladly in the gloom, 'hoping it might be so'.

But all this has only served to keep the embers glowing. Few have discovered the fire of the spirit or turned with true intent to find the 'secret place'. Now, in our practical age is arising a new concern to do this, to follow these leads that tug at the heart and track down their origin. Many of the young people are experimenting with drugs in their search for these deeper areas, and many among these, now finding this leads nowhere that is mentally satisfying, are turning to explore various fields of meditation.

Flights of fancy and mystical dreams have little appeal for the modern mind. Pretence will not be tolerated, reason must prevail, and the goal and the way to it must be defined in clear—if possible scientific—terms. In this framework the new concepts of meditation as a mental and logical method of inner penetration are taking on an important rôle.

A few years ago, meditation usually meant to most a 'religious' reflection. It suggested beside books and quiet gardens and the thoughtful writings of the mystics who had 'walked with God'. But in the East, meditation had long been practised as a mode of achieving consciousness on various levels of awareness, and the coming to the West of this teaching has brought about a new realization of the potential of this form of approach to that which is inner, higher or spiritual.

The science of meditation is primarily built on the concept of graded levels of life or consciousness or vibration. Seven major planes of life are spoken of in the Ageless Wisdom, each having seven degrees of density or vibration, and the function of meditation is to lead the conscious mind from stage to stage upon this inner stairway, from one level to another, gaining continually higher or subtler regions of awareness. This, briefly, is the essence of the true practice of meditation. It brings about a higher or greater consciousness and enables us to realize the more subjective realms.

True meditation is not simply an ecstatic experience, an emotional state of bliss or feeling of transcendency. Neither is it just an entry into a void. Some forms of meditation do, it is true, lead in these directions, but they will not assist us to take up our highest potential, and the processes that we should follow are those which are positive and utilize the higher powers of the mind.

This is why meditation is becoming almost a vogue today. It is being acknowledged as a means of *progressing in consciousness*, and many are feeling it can take them the next step forward. This stage is described by the Tibetan writer Djwhal Khul, and the turning point he depicts will be recognized by many:

As long as the polarization is purely physical or purely emotional, no need for meditation is ever felt. Even when the mental body is active, no urge arises until the man has run through many changes and many lives, has tasted the cup of pleasure and of pain through many incarnations, has sounded the depths of the life lived entirely for the lower self and found it unsatisfying. Then he begins to turn his thought to other things, to aspire to that which is unknown, to realize and sense within himself the pairs of opposites, and to contact within his consciousness possibilities and ideals undreamt of hitherto. He has come to a point where success, popularity and diverse gifts are his, and yet from their use he derives no content; always the urge within persists until the pain is so severe that the desire to reach out and up, to ascertain something and someone beyond, overcomes all obstacles. The man begins to turn within and to seek the source from whence he came. Then he begins to meditate, to ponder, to intensify his vibration until in process of time he garners the fruits of meditation.

Letters on Occult Meditation

In the past, prayer was the great life-line providing the link with what was felt to be Reality. It was the refuge turned to in adversity and danger, the method by which aid was entreated. It was the comfort of the needy, the strength of the fearful. It was also a true magnetic channel, for it tied the supplicant in with the greater powers to which he was appealing and along that 'life-line' energy flowed.

All this was, however, based upon faith that prayer would be heard and this premise does not satisfy the present intellectual outlook. Prayer—using the word in its specific sense —is also characterized by feeling, and people are today seeking to use their minds to approach Reality. They have learnt to distrust feeling. Prayer remains, therefore, a foundation for approach to the inner realms, but upon its up-turning attitude we superimpose meditation and gain the co-operation of the mind. We thus approach the unknown or super-conscious areas with intelligence as well as desire. These fields offer richer prospects if they are trodden knowingly, with all our capacities attuned, than they do if we simply hope blindly and receive, or seek to, with our eyes shut.

The difference between these two ways of approach becomes clearer if we consider the different spheres in which we live—physical, emotional and mental. There are subtler areas also, of which we are half aware, and we may presume that there are many more such regions beyond the scope of the human mind. In fact, the Ageless Wisdom, as mentioned earlier, speaks of seven such areas of Life in our Solar System and makes it clear that even all these are only the lowest level of cosmic Existence.

Such concepts may make the mind boggle, but they are not outrageous and if we look at the lower planes of life with which we are familiar, a logical pattern begins to appear. An old adage runs: 'As above, so below,' and the law of correspondences is one of the keys that unlocks the doors to the mysteries of the universe.

The different densities of the physical plane are well known to modern science. They are variously assessed and the subtler, etheric levels may not yet be fully understood or clarified, but we no longer think of physical matter as a solid block of substance. We know it vibrates in many different degrees and is, in fact, energy in its densest form of expression. Here, H. P. Blavatsky's definition of spirit and matter is of interest. She spoke of matter as spirit at its lowest point of manifestation, and spirit as matter in its highest evolutionary state. This thought opens up an entirely different approach to what we have up to now called 'God' or 'Divinity'—a Deity we have set apart in a mystical half of life separated off from manifesting form. It suggests that the domain of religion will, in the future, be far more closely linked with science, and out of this marriage we can expect to spring a whole new realization of both the form and divinity of the Life in which we belong.

In the area of emotion or feeling, the different 'grades' are equally well marked. Compare the lurid, heavy quality of fury, jealousy and hatred with love, idealism and aspiration. We can rise to realms of feeling that can hardly be described, as, for instance, when we are caught up by beauty or the power of music or the supreme ecstasy of devotion or mystical experience. Equally, we can sink into what we know to be the lowest levels of feeling—those motivated by physical demands or base and selfish drives. In between these two lies the full gamut of the emotional life—the idea of seven 'planes' or degrees of it does not over-stretch the imagination!

On the mental level, again, are the various differentiations, although here, as on all the planes of life it should be kept in mind that the different degrees or sub-planes are not marked by hard and fast dividing lines. In the world of thought it is perhaps more difficult to assess the various levels than in the physical and emotional spheres. But the three lowest areas are termed those of the 'concrete mind'. This is because we think in more or less 'concrete' terms in this area, that is, on objective and practical matters. In other words, on these levels thought is of a denser, heavier quality than is the abstract thought of the subtler planes.

It is said that we have a lower and a higher mind, the lower being affiliated with the personal life and the higher being the medium for abstract thought and approach to more subjective or superconscious spheres. This 'higher mind' offers us therefore, the means to penetrate beyond our usual 'ring-pass-not' of thinking. It is the instrument with which we pierce the shell of present knowing and break out to the fields of the superconscious—to realization on a wider scale.

Again, we shall be considering this aspect more fully when we come to the techniques of meditation. In fact, it must constitute our main underlying theme, for the interplay of the lower and higher parts of mind and our learning to use this higher faculty at will are the essence of the practice of meditation. For now, we are simply drawing a general picture. We might well say we are preparing the chart before setting out to explore the territory ahead—the uplands which our observations have convinced us hold the promise of things yet to be found.

One final point we should be as clear about as possible before starting on the project. What is our purpose, what our goal? Like the navigators of old, we can have only a general idea of direction when we set out to discover new domains, and even less do we know what will be found there. But on the purpose of our undertaking we can be more precise. The innate sense of an inner or higher or greater existence and the urge we consequently feel to proceed in its direction and discover more about it have already been seen to be strong underlying motivations and, without going into any philosophies of life, it is obviously of value to reach for understanding of this sensed 'reality' and achieve the highest stages of consciousness that we can. But there are further purposes to be borne in mind. If, through meditation, we learn to raise our level of thinking and balance the inner and the outer life, we act as conductors of this higher, more 'rarefied' atmosphere, as channels bringing it into the life of everyday. We recreate both ourselves and our surroundings.

The power of thought and the fact that thought is a very real form of energy are truths that are being realized fast. How great, then, is the opportunity that opens out before us as we stand at the opening of the higher mind! With that high instrument we can set up rapport with aspects and qualities which society desperately needs, and can help to build the New Age, which is talked about so much yet which, so far, is sadly lacking in spiritual direction.

Meditation, therefore, is not simply self-centred withdrawal. It can be a very real form of service and a positive and creative contribution to our fellow-men. It is a method of creating behind the scenes, as it were, of 'building without hands'. Everything which eventuates on earth has first been born in the world of the mind, and we should therefore remember that the new world of tomorrow is hourly being built by our thinking today.

It is also said that 'no man who strives for mastery of himself and aims at expanding his consciousness, but is having some effect—in ever widening spirals—on the world around him.' The power of thought, the power of prayer and invocation and the power of our own radiation are all essential elements in the contribution we are making, therefore, all the time to the world. The right use of these powers is consequently one of our highest challenges, and as we set out to explore the province of meditation, we have both the urge towards the 'Secret Place' and the fire of the heart that seeks to serve to take us forward.

The body is the Chariot, the senses (outer and inner) the Horses and the sense-objects the paths they travel. Those Horses are to be controlled by the Driver, *buddhi* by the aid of the reins of *manas*, the Lord or rider in the Chariot being the *Atman*, the Light of the One Self which pervades all things.

SRI KRISHNA PREM
The Yoga of the Kathopanishad

II · THE CHARIOTEER

Most people meditate without knowing it or giving their thinking this formal name. But all of us have some sort of contemplative ability, and all silent pondering on a problem, all direction of thought along a particular channel is, in a general sense, meditation.

The artist meditates to bring his inspiration into expression; the scientist meditates on his experiments and findings; the statesman meditates to solve the country's problems, the businessman to promote his trade, the doctor to find the nature of his patient's illness. In fact, we could almost use the old tag 'butcher, baker, candlestick-maker', for all new concepts, ideas and ideals, all truly constructive and effective action must first have been 'thought through' in the silent realms of the mind, and the more significant the achievement, the more mental preparation for it will have gone on 'behind the scenes'.

Meditation in this general sense builds a bridge between the inner and outer aspects of life, between higher or abstract thinking, ideas, inspiration, intuition and the outer form which such things take when they are put, through concrete mind creativity, into use on the physical plane. After all, the very construction of the word 'meditation' suggests that it is a bridging process between two halves of ourselves, a *mediatory* means by which two aspects or separated factors may be unified, and meditation is the means by which we reach from our concrete level thinking to the 'super' conscious, and build a usable channel between the two.

This is, perhaps, an over-simplification, and of course there are specific and more subjective forms of meditation which are far outside this general definition and beyond the average man's capacity; in fact, true meditation is a precise and difficult science requiring dedication of a high degree. But this preliminary definition shows how we are already working along meditative lines and laying the foundations for true communication with an inner or higher world whenever we face serious problems or matters of concern beyond the usual sphere of our more or less 'clockwork' thinking.

But as well as going on intermittently in this way, this 'bridge-building' is also taking place inevitably through the growth of our minds. The average mental capacity of people today is far greater than a few centuries ago, and far subtler levels of meaning and significance are now within our range. Much deeper thinking is therefore constantly brought into play, and more subjective elements influence our reactions. Also, we are continually searching for new knowledge, which is widening our field of awareness and bridging into worlds not yet known.

This expansion is obviously a progress we are destined to make, and it is taking place continually in spite of ourselves. But we can linger overlong on it and various dangers are then apt to raise their heads. One of the most prevalent of these at present is the very fact of our mental prowess, which builds a maze around us from which it is hard to escape. Our minds love being active and as they get bigger and better we head into complexities of many kinds. The mind will work like a Trojan in obedience to any desire; the ancient urge of accretion, for example, is fed like a fighting cock today by our technical ability—which could almost be called the 'religion' of the lower mental life. More and more, as our restless minds take over, we get caught up by distractions which, like the roundabouts on a fairground, keep us in endless motion, yet never achieve very much.

If we are wise to it at this point, we can assume a commanding rôle and train the mind and make use of it in whatever way we decide. But often enough it gets out of control and is off like a runaway horse, with us a helpless rider, before we have realized it. The problem of how we use our minds, of whether they build or burn our bridges—or whether, in fact, they use *us*—comes back at root to the question of who decides? Who runs our lives? Who is the controller?

We have spoken of outer and inner worlds; we have also outer and inner selves with which we inhabit these two places. Mystery veils the inner Self, just as it guards the inner world, and the interdependence of these two selves or 'halves' of our being is one of the agelong problems of mankind. But the outer self—of which we know more and which we will, therefore, look at first—also has its mysteries; it is complex in its constitution as well as nature, and not as clearly understood as might at first be expected.

It is made up of physical body, emotions and mind, each of which has its characteristics, yet none of which is truly the 'I'. This, when we come to look at it, is obvious; we are not our bodies, minds or emotions—we act, think, feel *through* them. Yet we do not always remember the differentiation and are apt to become identified with any temporary overriding urge or thought or feeling.

We may be surprised, in fact, at what is going on if we set up the habit of watching our actions and motives, and standing as the 'observer', detachedly in the wings. We soon see that different parts of our selves are behaving in different ways. One part may be tired or lazy, while another is over-active and fretting to get ahead; one part may be rebellious, while another is quite content; one may crave to pursue a certain line of action, while another is afraid of it or prefers something else. The mind may persistently worry, or the emotional nature be afraid, while all the time the self is saying it is quite without foundation.

We are certainly not always in agreement with the different parts of ourselves, and spend a lot of our time trying to check their headstrong ways. These elements or aspects are, therefore, obviously not our 'selves'. Like a harassed parent plagued by a bunch of children, we are plucked at by our various parts, and are often pulled in different directions so that, if we are not prepared for it, we get torn and worn by their conflicts and our power to control them is then undermined.

To meet this situation, who then is the 'self', the 'I', the *controlling* consciousness? The first part of the answer begins to appear when we realize we are not our senses or our bodies, and that neither are we our minds. Once we recognize these as elements of our make-up, we are confirming the independence of the observing self and are on the way to true control of our equipment instead of being at its beck and call.

This position is frequently depicted in the epic teachings of the ancient Vedas in the symbology of the charioteer with his chariot and horses. There are various versions of the analogy, but perhaps the most helpful for our purpose is the picture of the charioteer as the self, the chariot as the life he is leading and the horses as the mental, emotional and physical aspects or 'bodies' which take his chariot forward. The analogy goes further, and we find Patanjali equating the reins—with which the charioteer controls his horses—with thoughts, the medium through which the self communicates with his threefold nature.

Plato uses this symbology of the charioteer also and

remarks of the horses: 'As might be expected, there is a great deal of trouble in managing them'! The analogy is helpful and it is well worth giving it some thought, for it clarifies the different rôles of our various aspects and emphasizes the need for the self to be in command—the charioteer *in control* of the energies harnessed to his chariot.

All this may seem obvious, but who does not know times when we lose control and one or other of our 'horses' gets out of hand? On these occasions we are apt to forget about our independent position; we become identified with the—temporarily—overwhelming urge and are swept along wherever it wills, a sad example of abdication!

The analogy of the horses emphasizes the fact that these three aspects of our make-up are definite forms of *energy*, and recognition of this puts us on our guard, for we have, literally, three separate types of energy to handle. Each of these elements has its own characteristics and qualities—vices and virtues that we have to curb or use; each of them has its own drives and tendencies, motives and demands, and these, again, we learn to know and handle—offset or utilise. Each may pull in a different direction; not always, for example, do emotions go hand in hand with thought. Then at another time, thought and feeling will gang up together on such things as fear, anxiety and depression. Then they pull us down unwonted paths and we are hard put to it to check them and reassume control.

In fact, as charioteer we have to perform a considerable balancing act. We must stand poised, in charge, but yet we are dependent on the energies or elements at our disposal. Their various pulls must be assessed and adjusted, and ever our vision harnessed to—though not weighed down by—their potential 'horsepower'. In all these things, the strong hand of the one in charge is vitally needed, the guiding hand of the charioteer who holds the reins and, standing poised above his horses, sees the road that they must follow.

An exercise to help in establishing this attitude of the 'observer' and controller is outlined at the end of this chapter. Its regular use will be found a valuable aid both to recognition of the *self* at the centre and to lessening the grip that the lower nature exerts. We begin to get the habit of standing more detachedly at the centre and of handling our various aspects from that point if we take this stand deliberately, and consciously affirm that we are the self.

But we have not yet fully answered the question 'who am I?' and we must at least attempt to reach a more comprehensive picture. We cannot, however, expect to learn the whole story, even in a life-time, because the inner as well as outer 'halves' of our being are involved—the infinite and eternal as well as the immediate and individual. But it is a story that is not new to us. It has been told in a thousand folk tales and fables, epics and myths, allegories and fairy stories and, of course, it forms the core of most religions. The theme of the two 'selves' or the Soul and its persona, King and servant, greater and lesser consciousness (to use more current terms) recurs insistently in one form or another in all kinds of teachings all over the world.

> From their number and the variety of incident and of details in which the leading idea is embodied, we may infer that the conception of an external soul is one which has had a powerful hold on the minds of men at an early stage of history. For folk-tales are a faithful reflection of the world as it appeared to the primitive mind; and we may be sure that any idea which commonly occurs in them, must once have been an ordinary article of belief. FRAZER
> *The Golden Bough*

In the ancient Vedas we find it referred to as the 'two birds'—the 'Supreme and the individual Souls'—

Vast is THAT, Its form unthinkable . . .
Yet it rests in the heart's heart.

Krishna affirmed it in the well-known words: 'Having
pervaded the entire universe with a fragment of Myself, I
remain.' And in the parables of Jesus it was taught again and
again—the Lord always in a far country, his servant in the
vineyard. It was given precise point in the parable of the
leaven placed in the three measures of meal and the story of
the five, three and one talents is based on the same theme.

Yet despite it being a universal message all down the
ages—and the poets particularly have cried of it from their
hearts—it still remains not fully told, a secret story that we
have to discover each in our own way, outside the realm of
words and beyond our present circumscribed conceptions.
We only know that an echo of the higher Self lingers in our
consciousness—like the half-memory of the inner world
which we noted earlier some can recall. The 'I', the fragment
of the Greater Consciousness, retains, deep in it, the vibration
of the 'Super Self' from which it came. We cannot lose this,
although sometimes it may be deeply hidden; like a homing
missile drawn back to its station by the beam to which it
responds, we must obey the urge to break our fetters, widen
our awareness, reach back to the greater realms. A human
being is said to be 'an immortal Existence, an eternal God, a
portion of Infinity'. Is there any wonder that we are victims
of a 'divine discontent'?

The outer self is not in an easy position. We must bear full
responsibility for the elements in our charge, yet we are not
independent. We still owe obedience to the higher Self,
which is recognized sometimes through the 'voice of conscience' but which generally remains beyond our reach. In
this situation we have to live in the world, but ever remember we are not of it; must carry out our daily tasks, yet never
lose the sense of our divinity; and, circumscribed by hard,

cold facts and material existence, still foster the capacity to soar, serene, above them.

Conflict is said to be the means by which humanity finds harmony, and perhaps it is, therefore, this very struggle between the two pulls of the two existences—the outer and inner—that eventually induces a kind of divine desperation. With this we rise up, reaching for the higher Self, and affirm at last, despite all obstacles, our spiritual identity. The number of those who have reached this point is legion and they do not need to be named. But they are the witnesses of what we sense, they have pioneered the way that we shall eventually go and we need not lack encouragement.

This brings us back to the subject of meditation, because here we have a direct and practical method of reaching towards and penetrating this 'super' conscious region, of extending our boundaries and kindling the latent spark in us of the Flame of Divinity. We will go into the deeper—or higher—aspects of this in the following chapters. But we should first make sure that we have come to an understanding of our 'self' and have a sound sense of the 'I' as the coordinating and controlling consciousness which *uses* its threefold nature.

We might also, while recognizing the regency of the self, usefully make some assessments of the values and discrepancies of our three elements. In this way we shall be able to recognize more speedily when any of them are carrying us away, and we shall be able to harness them more skilfully into an integrated whole to fulfil our purposes and carry out our rôle.

If the following exercise seems simple, that is all to the good. It means that we are standing as wise observers and can quickly move on to further fields. If it seems yet to be difficult, then we should work at it with intention. We shall soon reap reward and find we are beginning to stand as the charioteer, our team reined in, our balance held and our eyes directed towards our destiny.

Exercise in dis-identification and
recognition of the central self

I Take up a comfortable, relaxed position with closed
   eyes. Breathe quietly.

   AFFIRM: 'I *have* a body but *I am not* my body. My
   body may be in different conditions of
   health or sickness; it may be rested or tired,
   but it is not my real "I". My body is my
   precious instrument of experience and of
   action, but it is only an instrument. I treat
   it well; I seek to keep it in good health, but
   it *is not* myself. I *have* a body, but *I am not*
   my body.'

II AFFIRM: 'I *have* emotions, but *I am not* my emotions.
   They are countless, contradictory, changing,
   and yet I know that I always remain I,
   my-self, in times of hope or despair, in joy
   or pain, in a state of irritation or calm.
   Since I can observe, understand and judge
   my emotions, and then increasingly
   dominate, direct and utilize them, it is
   evident that they *are not myself*. I have
   emotions, but *I am not* my emotions.'

   'I *have* desires, but *I am not* my desires.
   They, too, are changeable and contradictory,
   with alternations of attraction and repulsion.
   I *have* desires but *they are not* myself.'

III AFFIRM: 'I *have* an intellect, but *I am not* my intellect.
   It is more or less developed and active; it is
   undisciplined but teachable; it is an organ of
   knowledge in regard to the outer world as

well as the inner; but *it is not myself.* I *have* an intellect, but *I am not* my intellect.'

iv   After this dis-identification of the I from its physical, emotional and mental vehicles, recognize and affirm:

'*I am a centre of pure Self-consciousness.*
I am a centre of *Will*, capable of mastering, directing and using all my psychological processes and my physical body. *I am* the constant and unchanging *Self.*'

This exercise is based on one of the techniques given in *Psychosynthesis*, by Dr Roberto Assagioli, and is given here with the kind permission of the author and the Psychosynthesis Research Foundation, New York.

A man must have a sort of intelligence of the Absolute. . . . a recollection of those things which the soul beheld when it was in the company of God, an escape from relative being in the apprehension of true Being. In this, the mind of the philosopher alone has wings. To the extent of its enlightenment, it recollects those things in which Divinity abides.

PLATO

III · HIGH AND WIDE

The eye, it is said, must be ahead of the foot, vision must range beyond capability. Were it not so, how should we discover which way to go forward? For this reason we shall look at the *super* conscious in this chapter, so that we have an idea of where we are going, of the regions—or fastnesses—we hope to explore, before starting on the humbler task of the groundwork of meditation.

This may seem to the cautious minded the wrong way round to go about our project, but wings are gained for our laggard feet if we first look at the goals ahead and see their logic and potential. The announcement of a mystery is always a signal to human nature to rise from its common lot and strive to find an answer. An unknown land is a clarion call for exploration, and the power of a challenge always seems to have a magical effect on our all too slothful substance.

Vision, too, has immense pulling power. It is no vague or impractical thing in its true exemplification, but acts magnetically upon our secret centre, urging us forward—awakening perhaps some hidden knowledge of truth, or life, or divinity? As if we threw a rope up to a pinnacle we wished to scale, so vision offers a life-line whereby we can reach beyond the confines of our present consciousness, knowing a glorious moment of communication with another dimension, of cognisance of a world beyond the four square walls of common life.

Vision is a potential energy in us all. Mentally it is creative, emotionally it is stimulating; physically it harnesses our forces to our purpose, and it works practically and logically through our sense of 'something higher'—that inner sense that generates all our upward progress. The idea of seeing the vision and materializing it runs like a golden thread through all mystical writings. It is always connected with spiritual achievement, attainment of a high goal, recognition of that which lies ahead and which is at the heart of all spiritual adventure. In the past it has been prostituted often by excessive emotionalism, but vision and emotion have no need to be bed-fellows and the mental polarization of today should bring about perceptive and scientific use of this quiet power of promise and objective.

It is, therefore, something to be fostered, cultivated, even indulged in, lest we crystallize and petrify in our twilight world. The psalmist's declaration 'I will lift up mine eyes unto the hills' was a realistic and objective statement of intention and a recognition that vision is the opening of a doorway through which first we see and then, when the hidden powers have flooded through sufficiently, we eventually make our way.

Perhaps some small conceit—the outgrowth of a needed confidence—also supports us, making us think that we are little gods and all things are possible. Hope also dangles carrots before our eyes. But let us not turn down any aids that we can muster, for the struggle of the exiled soul to find its way back to its all-knowing Parent is no mean adventure. We need to call upon all our resources and marshall all the help we can. Indeed, this particular project of finding the way from the self to the Self could hardly be undertaken if we had no vision with which to look ahead. Vision and inspiration, too, go hand in hand. The one, having offered the vista, the other pours forth its gifts. So we get a double shot in the arm if we raise our eyes sufficiently, and must carefully guard these gifts of the spirit to feed us in leaner times.

The possibility of penetrating consciously into the usually super conscious regions is well documented. Illumination is an acknowledged stage of spiritual progress, following the stages of awakening and purification. In the East it is commonly spoken of—and known—as the reward of long and rigid self-discipline and effort. But it is also beginning to be studied from the more scientific psychological angle and 'peak experiences' are recognized by those in the forefront of the new psychiatry today, 'lived experiences' of high states of awareness resulting from endeavour to reach spiritual understanding or attain a fuller or deeper life.

An interesting study was made as long ago as the end of the last century by Dr Richard Maurice Bucke of cases in which there was evidence of illumination. He gathered a surprising amount of material describing the experience from the writings of those who had achieved this state, and also those who had observed the effects and changes brought about in the person concerned.

These experiences all had a mental, emotional and physical effect. They were all characterized by an intense sense of unification or universal oneness, and realization of the pervasion of God. This is epitomized in what are said to be the Buddha's spontaneous words at the moment of enlightenment:

Wonder of wonders! Intrinsically all living beings are Buddhas, endowed with wisdom and virtue, but because their minds have become inverted through delusive thinking they fail to perceive this.

These words are variously recorded in the Buddhist scriptures, but we may take this as a fair interpretation.

Dr Bucke used the term 'Cosmic Consciousness' for the various stages of illumination, a term which perhaps rather exaggerates the possibilities of earthbound human beings, but which, nevertheless, conveys the 'super-individual' realization reached. He speaks of greater and lesser or 'imperfect' attainment of illumination and describes the state as a 'consciousness of the cosmos, that is, of the life and order of the universe'. Along with this awareness occurs, he writes,

> an intellectual enlightenment or illumination which alone would place the individual on a new plane of existence—would make him almost a member of a new species. To this is added a state of moral exaltation, an indescribable feeling of elevation, elation and joyousness, and a quickening of the moral sense, which is fully as striking and more important both to the individual and to the race as is the enhanced intellectual power. With these come what might be called a sense of immortality, a consciousness of eternal life, not a conviction that he shall have this, but the consciousness that he has it already.
>
> *Cosmic Consciousness, p. 3*

There are many well-known stories of this high experience of light, such as Moses' descent from Mount Sinai with the tablets of the Commandments 'when he wist not that the skin of his face shone or sent forth beams', so that the children of Israel 'were afraid to come nigh him'. And all know of St Paul's experience on the road to Damascus. We cannot go into the many instances of which there are details which leave no doubt of their validity. But quite apart from the well-known examples, the mystical 'translations' and experiences of divine ecstasy recorded in all religious annals, Bucke lists many who, without any particular 'religious impulsion', have reached these states of awareness consciously and given full and careful accounts of the experience.

One of these was Pascal. From a document he wrote in duplicate, which was found after his death hidden carefully in the lining of his doublet, and now in the Bibliotheque Nationale, Paris, we have evidence of his experience of a supreme subjective light—'Fire'—he wrote in large letters. It was an experience which lasted about two hours and was followed by a supreme sense of liberation, joy and the grandeur of the human soul. As with many of the others known to have had illumination, his life was changed from then on. He practically retired into seclusion and most would agree that his most brilliant work was produced after this.

Poets, we know, have frequently written of these high glimpses of another state. For example, Wordsworth's lines, written at Tintern Abbey:

. . . That serene and blessed mood
In which the affections gently lead us on,—
Until, the breath of this corporeal frame
And even the motion of our human blood
Almost suspended, we are laid asleep
In body, and become a living soul.

The interesting suggestion is put forward by one school of thought that Shakespeare's Sonnets were, in reality, addressed to his own Soul, or the 'Cosmic Sense', and express the longing of the exiled self, embedded in the consciousness of the personality, to achieve union with that which he knew to be his true complement. We have, perhaps, unthinkingly accepted the affirmations, pictures and descriptions of the poets and great writers down the centuries as simply flights of fancy and expressions of their supreme sense of beauty. But they are more than that, and worthy of deeper examination. In a great many instances they indicate the tangible and definite experience of the subtler background of the outer life.

Day seemed to be added to day as if he who is able had adorned the heavens with another sun.

wrote Dante, and his words are echoed almost exactly in Walt Whitman's *Leaves of Grass*:

> . . . one instant,
> Another sun, ineffable full-dazzles me,
> And all the orbs I knew, and brighter, unknown orbs:
> One instant of the future land, Heaven's land.

Both men knew the illumination of the higher planes of consciousness and Whitman referred to it many times. For example:

> The soul emerges, and all statements, churches,
> sermons, melt away like vapours. Alone, and silent
> thought, and awe, and aspiration—and then the *interior*
> *consciousness*, like a hitherto unseen inscription, in magic
> ink, beams out its wondrous lines to the sense. Bibles
> may convey and priests expound, but it is exclusively
> for the noiseless operation of one's isolated *Self* to enter
> the pure ether of veneration, reach the divine levels, and
> commune with the unutterable.
>
> *Democratic Vistas*

Here is no emotional ecstasy, but a calm and clear appraisal of a mental penetration into super-normal areas or planes of realization. In another passage from the same work, Whitman expresses lucidly the sense of Universal Life which is such a characteristic of the attainment of realization on these levels:

> And lo! to the consciousness of the soul, the permanent identity, the thought, the something, before which the magnitude even of Democracy, art, literature, etc., dwindles, becomes partial, measurable—something that fully satisfies (which these do not). That something is the *All* and the idea of *All*, with the accompanying idea of eternity, and of itself, the soul, buoyant, indestructible, sailing Space forever, visiting every region, as a ship the sea. And again lo! the pulsations in all matter, all spirit, throbbing forever—the eternal beats, eternal systole and dyastole of life in things— wherefrom I feel and know that death is not the ending, as we thought, but rather the beginning—and that nothing ever is or can be lost, nor even die, nor soul nor matter.

If we look further back in history, we find a 'classic' example of those who have achieved these levels in Plotinus who, although he complained that 'to write is always irksome to me', wrote this illuminating passage in a letter to Flaccus:

> Knowledge has three degrees—opinion, science, illumination . . . You ask, how can we know the Infinite? I answer, not by reason. It is the office of reason to distinguish and define. The Infinite, therefore, cannot be ranked among its objects. You can only apprehend the Infinite by a faculty superior to reason, by entering into a state in which you are your finite self no longer—in which the divine essence is

communicated to you. This is ecstasy. It is the liberation of your mind from its finite consciousness. Like only can apprehend like; when you thus cease to be finite, you become one with the Infinite. In the reduction of your soul to its simplest self, its divine essence, you realize this union, this identity.

But this sublime condition is not of permanent duration. It is only now and then that we can enjoy this elevation above the limits of the body and the world. I myself have realized it but three times as yet, and Porphyry hitherto not once. All that tends to purify and elevate the mind will assist you in this attainment, and facilitate the approach and the recurrence of these happy intervals.

Over-emphasis, must not be placed, however, on the attainment of above normal or phenomenal states of awareness. The long path of meditation is a process of steady, step by step building in consciousness, and such experiences as those just mentioned cannot be expected until we are well along the way. In the meantime we may take comfort in remembering Porphyry!

True arrival at these levels is also a matter of evolutionary growth, which brings about naturally—if slowly—the gradual expansion of consciousness. Illumination cannot be attained until we are sufficiently evolved or elevated in ourselves, for, as Plotinus pointed out, 'like only can apprehend like'. To put it another way, our own vibration must be sufficiently heightened to permit—and render possible—recognition of the higher vibrations of the subtler planes.

This puts such revelations and experiences into their true proportion. They are simply evidence of stages on the way, stages of varying degrees, and before any of them can be truly known and assimilated we have to put in the groundwork, that is, go through the processes known in mystical terms as *Awakening* and *Purification*. We may prefer to call these stages *Recognition* and *Refinement*; that is, recognition of the *self* (for 'Knowledge of the self is the absolute and all-essential basis for knowledge of the Truth', writes Paul Brunton, whom we may conclude from his writings speaks from experience), and refinement or transmutation of our substance—physical, emotional and mental. But the fundamental task entailed remains the same and no true experience of the higher regions, it must be reiterated, can be expected until these earlier stages have been achieved, at least to a certain degree.

Lest we begin to get discouraged by the seeming far distance of these high achievements, rather than encouraged by the pioneering of those who have gone ahead, it may be wise to turn now to modern psychology, which has some encouragement to give. The more forward looking in this field are realizing not only the existence of a higher 'Self', but the hidden power which this can exert upon the individual. In fact, as with the discovery of certain of the planets, it is the effect, or pull, of some unknown influence which has called attention to the existence of a hidden source of power or attraction.

From observation, if not from personal experience, therefore, these 'supra states' are acknowledged as occurring occasionally and constituting a supreme crisis in the life of the individual concerned, who frequently does not understand what is taking place and has no knowledge of how to handle the experience. These states of heightened awareness, called by Maslow and others 'peak experiences', are not, of course, in the category of the illuminations referred to earlier in this chapter, but they are what might be called indications of higher sensitivity and attunement. As such they need to be understood and worked with intelligently, particularly because their incidence is increasing with the rapidly evolving mental ability and greater awareness of mankind today.

In earlier ages these experiences were more easily accepted; the background of religion was sufficiently strong to give the individual a 'frame of reference', and he more readily and completely attuned himself with devotion to the enlightenment of higher influences with which he came in contact. Today, young people are frequently worried by the sense of the subjective and the higher or inner promptings that sometimes come to them. They have no knowledge of subtler planes and little belief in spirituality to support them, and therefore cannot understand the situation in which they sometimes find themselves—one of genuine attunement to higher vibrations.

Pioneers in this field are beginning to speak of 'Height Psychology' and to make a study of the superconscious functions, such as intuition, inspiration and higher creativity. This is also called 'Spiritual Psychosynthesis' by Dr Roberto Assagioli, one of the most eminent in this particular field, and at this point it might be helpful to study the diagram from his book, *Psychosynthesis*, given on the opposite page.

This diagram will help to clarify the various regions referred to in our study of meditation and, consequently, the possible trajectory of the conscious self, the 'I', the 'observer'. It indicates what might be called the psychological constitution of the human being, and while any two-dimensional chart of such a 'pluridimensional' factor must necessarily be fractional and inadequate, it serves to give an approximate representation of the fields of the psychological life, in other words, the different areas in which we function, from which we receive motivation, impression, impulses and impacts of all kinds, and to which we may expect to penetrate. From this diagram, therefore, we shall perhaps be able to form a clearer concept of what we are about when we undertake meditation, and realize that it is a much more scientific process than the old idea of it as simply a religious exercise and a little while spent in negative reflection.

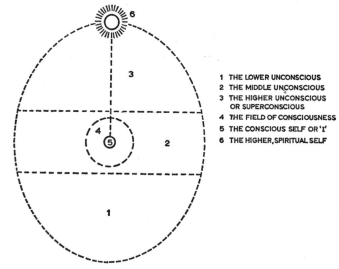

1 THE LOWER UNCONSCIOUS
2 THE MIDDLE UNCONSCIOUS
3 THE HIGHER UNCONSCIOUS
  OR SUPERCONSCIOUS
4 THE FIELD OF CONSCIOUSNESS
5 THE CONSCIOUS SELF OR 'I'
6 THE HIGHER, SPIRITUAL SELF

Chart of the Spheres of Consciousness

From this chart we see that the conscious 'I', the part of our selves which is in charge and which we have seen in the previous chapter must become the observer and controller, constitutes the central point of the field of consciousness. This, in turn, is situated in what is here called the 'middle unconscious', in other words, the area which is most easily accessible to the conscious mind and where our various experiences are assimilated. The lower unconscious will be readily understood as the area of the deeper and more primitive urges, drives, complexes and motivations, and the region where lie dormant our various repressions.

Above the 'middle unconscious' we come to the 'higher unconscious', or *superconscious*, (3) and from this region we receive our higher intuitions, inspirations and spiritual impulses. This is the area we seek to penetrate in meditation. Here we contact influences and energies of subtler or more spiritual vibration, and it is in this area that we find the higher Self or Soul and eventually, having developed the ability to identify with it, may achieve illumination.

Of the reality of this 'True Self' or permanent centre, Assagioli writes:

There are various ways by means of which the reality of the Self can be ascertained. There have been many individuals who have achieved, more or less temporarily, a conscious realization of the Self that for them has the same degree of certainty as is experienced by an explorer who has entered a previously unknown region. Such statements can be found in Bucke's *Cosmic Consciousness*, in Ouspensky's *Tertium Organum*, in Underhill's *Mysticism*, and in other books. The awareness of the Self can also be achieved through the use of certain psychological methods, among which are Jung's 'process of individuation', Desoille's 'Rêve éveillé', techniques of Raja Yoga, etc.

Then we have the corroboration of such philosophers as Kant, and Herbart, who made a clear distinction between the empirical ego and the noumenical or real Self. This Self is above, and unaffected by, the flow of the mind-stream or by bodily conditions; and the personal conscious self should be considered merely as its reflection, its 'projection' in the field of the personality. At the present stage of psychological investigation little is definitely known concerning the Self, but the importance of this synthesising centre well warrants further research.

. . . all the superior manifestations of the human psyche, such as creative imagination, intuition, aspiration, genius, are facts which are as real and as important as are the conditioned reflexes, and therefore are susceptible to research and treatment just as scientifically . . .

Psychosynthesis, pp. 19 and 193

From all this we see that meditation is no vague or negative entry into nebulous spheres. It is a positive method of working in consciousness and penetrating so far undiscovered regions of the superconscious. It is a means of utilizing the power of the mind vertically instead of horizontally—of pioneering upwards instead of contriving and constructing in endless 'dead pan' circles on the planes of our environment.

The chart on p. 39 can provide a general map as we set out on the adventure of meditation, but it is rather like one of the mariner's charts of old which only indicates the coast-lines crudely and does not give the hills and valleys of the terrain in between. These we have to trace for ourselves as we slowly make our way through the wide country of the mental planes—the uplands that will bring us eventually to the court of the higher Self—the place we sense in higher moments to be our 'home'.

One of the key factors is that we can only accomplish this as *integrated* units, that is, individuals with the three 'horses' of our chariot harnessed and co-ordinated, and the conscious self, the 'I' well poised as the observer, director, controller, charioteer. To quote Assagioli again—'It is in the co-operation and synthetic use of *all* human functions that success—either in cognition or in action—can be achieved.'

This means that all parts of our selves contribute to true meditation. Not only must the mind be addressed to it, but the emotional nature through its orientation and desire, or dedication, and the physical brain cells, too, must serve obediently. The stages on the Path referred to earlier—Awakening or Recognition and Purification or Transmutation—are the preparation for this, the needed preliminary steps. They serve to stir us from complacency, to bring about an upward effort, to refine, and elevate the threefold nature and render it, as a whole, sufficiently attuned.

All this is not done in a day, but we can take heart in that much of it will already be behind us, or we would not now have the urge to address ourselves to the search for the higher Self. Perfection and full triumph may be a long way off. We may make assays and then be pulled back, the prey of our substance. But *effort* is a first essential, and the assertion of some discipline upon the lower nature not only serves to control it, but affirms our individual right as the one at the centre with a higher sense of direction and an inner, subjective goal.

In the next chapters we shall be going more fully into techniques and aspects of meditation which will serve as 'sailing orders'. But before that, let us take stock of our situation, carefully, in our hearts, seeing the field that lies before us, and recalling how many have found their way into its distant places, leaving for us signposts although it may not yet be a well-trodden way.

To vision, then, we can add some evidence. That of others can never, of course, be the same as the witness of our own eyes, but that they have succeeded in making these penetrations must give us confidence, must strengthen and inspire. We can very well conceive that it is no mere flight of fancy that we are embarked upon, but a tried and sound pathway—known since ancient times—which may lead some to Illumination, but all of us towards our Souls.

Silence is in truth the attribute of God, and those who seek Him from that side invariably learn that meditation is not the dream but the reality of life; not its illusion but its truth; not its weakness but its strength.

JAMES MARTINEAU

IV · DOWN TO EARTH

Having spread our wings and caught vicariously a little of the vision that others have seen, we must now get down to the spade-work of building our own silent path. There are many kinds of meditation and many methods are taught, but the basic stages are much the same, and since this is more or less a guide-book for newcomers, it will perhaps be most useful to take a look first at the general preliminaries and the problems which are usually met.

A place in which to meditate is often difficult to find today, especially for young people with families. It may well be impossible to find somewhere quiet, far less any place to be alone. But at least a certain degree of seclusion must be achieved—a place both in time and space where we shall not normally be interrupted and can at least expect to have a certain time of comparative peace. This is important because, if we fear interruption all the time and are listening to protect ourselves from surprise, true concentration will not be possible, and we cannot hope to achieve much more than address ourselves to the higher forces and repeat some form of mantram or prayer.

However, this is a universal problem; we must not be deterred by it, but must do the best we can in the given situation, knowing that cloistered solitude is not the rule today. It has, in fact, been said that the extraverted life of the present day aspirant, with its noise and stress and lack of seclusion, constitutes one of his major testings, and that modern 'disciples' must be able to lead the 'dual life', that is, hold the inner orientation while fulfilling the outer demands.

We must therefore build our private oratory where and when we can, in hidden moments and in secret ways, for few will be able to take the time they would like for meditation. If we have no room that is private, even a corner can become a place of meditation if we use it regularly and perhaps keep there one or two objects which will anchor its special purpose and preserve its atmosphere. Books, for instance, are packed with the potency of the thoughts in them, and if they are of the right type, they are therefore conducive to thought and reflection. A picture, too, can have a tangible influence, inspiring or tranquillizing or giving a spiritual stimulus; so, also, can some symbolic object, like a figure of the Buddha in meditation, or a candle, or a flower or a joss-stick burning —whatever suggests to us, individually, the inner life we are seeking to attune with will help to create the atmosphere in which we can meditate best.

Such things can carry a quality or vibration which not only helps to put us in the right frame of mind, but helps to condition the whole environment and 'lift' the feel of the room. But if it is not possible to have such aids—and some may feel no need of them anyway—then the act of meditating in the same place daily will be found to build up a helpful atmosphere. An aura of meditative quality will gradually begin to grow, so that when we come in to it to start our work, we can feel its protective and directive power. This is the same as the feel we get—on a much greater scale—when we enter an ancient church and sense the centuries of prayer.

So far as it is possible then, it is good to meditate in the same place as a general rule. Of course we can use the time in trains and buses and all kinds of moments snatched from the clutches of the day—and this is of inestimable value. But for the quiet practice of inner withdrawal and the learning to build a true approach to the 'Oversoul', it will help to have a special place which we keep for vertical thought and fill with the vibration of more subjective realms. If we read and study in this place as well as meditate, it will quickly become a sanctuary to which we can retreat, where strength and solace will enfold us and we loose off the world whenever we feel the need.

The idea of creating a 'place' for meditation may sound like too much mystical devotion, but it is, in fact, a suggestion that is spiritually sound, that is, founded on inner or subtle law. Atmosphere is conditioned by thought, and objects can carry a spiritual vibration. This has been known by the custodians of all the great religions. Misuse of forms has sometimes led to their being discarded, but their use as an aid to spiritual approach has been understood and utilized since Moses directed the Israelites to build the Tabernacle, and the temples of even earlier religions were erected.

But while all these things help to turn attention upwards, too much emphasis should not be laid on objects or surroundings. However magnetic they may be, they can only form a background in which we do the work. Some people find it helpful to meditate out of doors, in a place of beauty, in the midst of nature and away from the 'world'. Such places can certainly give a sense of freedom and oneness with the Infinite, and the ethers are clearer for meditating when we get away from the impact of everyone's thought. But others sometimes find this too diffusing for specific meditation and the sense of expansion not conducive to focussed work.

It also holds another subtle trap. We can be caught up by

beauty too much, and may mistake the rapture it induces for true penetration into spiritual spheres. It is important to recognize the difference between absorption through beauty or devotion or the transporting effect of music and other such stimuli to the emotions, and the practice of meditation as a process of gaining greater consciousness with the aid of the *mind*. This mistake is often made by the beginner and he must look hard at himself to make sure he is keeping rightly balanced between heart aspiration and mind rationale, with neither having too much sway.

We shall go into this more fully later on, when considering the different kinds of meditation and techniques and methods of approach. But the beginner should be clear from the out-set that the aim is not emotional exaltation, nor is it unthinking absorption in the Infinite, and beauty—for all its wonder—must not be allowed to carry us off in its arms.

The time at which we meditate will also have to conform to the individual life pattern and to whenever—if ever—quiet may prevail. But generally speaking, the golden time for addressing ourselves to the inner life is the start of the day. For one thing, the early hours are quieter; the ethers are not yet filled with movement and noise. The dawn hour, before the world awakes, is a magical time for communication between the two areas of our existence—inner and outer, source and manifestation, spiritual and physical, energy and form. It is said that sleep was forbidden during the dawn hour in the early Mystery Schools, and that all neophytes had to be absorbed in their spiritual exercises when the sun appeared.

Another reason for making meditation the first act of the day is that our minds are then comparatively still. They are not yet besieged by the thousand and one demands that meet us once the day begins, and not yet stirred into the innumerable streams of thought that intrude upon all efforts to meditate if concentration is not strong. For beginners especially, therefore, this is the most propitious time for the mind to remain steady and obedient to the will.

An even more important reason for early morning meditation may not be apparent when we first begin. It is the fact that it constitutes an act of orientation and an intake of energy that stabilizes and fortifies for the day. It puts us in touch with inner forces that affirm our spiritual standing, and once we are a little practised, it seems to place the cloak of the Soul upon our shoulders before we meet the rigours of the day.

If morning meditation is not possible, then evening provides the next best time. The sunset hour is an interlude which holds a special potency of its own. It is said that certain chemical changes occur as the sun goes down and night takes over from the pulse of day. Certainly it is a time when the tempo slows down, when the breathing of the world seems to alter and the great Systemic Rhythm makes itself felt throughout all kingdoms of nature, a rhythm which all but men obey. At this hour the mind turns more easily to an interior quiet and attunes with the magical transforming quality that slips at dusk across the world.

The story is told by one of the Eastern Masters that the World Teacher—known in the West as the Christ—daily stands under a great pine tree at the hour of sunset, and pours out his blessing to the world. Perhaps, therefore, when we tune in for meditation—or even a minute's recollection—as the sun goes down, we catch a fragment of a spiritual emanation sweeping across the earth to every listening ear.

The value of rhythm should be recognized too. Human beings are strangely addicted to habit, and 'grooves' of varying value are quickly imprinted on the subconscious mind, or to be more precise and quoting from the diagram on p. 39 (Chapter III), the middle and lower regions of the unconscious. In common with most of nature's creatures we, therefore, easily slip into patterns of behaviour. Our minds, emotions, brain cells soon react according to how we have 'programmed' them, and work automatically along these lines from then on with less imposition of discipline or directive by the central self.

This means that if we 'programme' habits that develop the spiritual life, we can cash in on this natural tendency and save ourselves considerable circumnabulation through reluctances and conflicts in our various parts. The habit of early morning meditation could usefully be the first of such 'programming' attempted, and a short time of experiment will soon begin to repay. The habit of turning our attention upwards, of addressing our hearts to the good, soon becomes, a built-in rhythm that reorientates us every day. It has, in fact, been said by one of the great teachers of the East that this habit can 're-polarize the entire lower man' and set him firmly on the path of the disciple.

But no matter what hour is decided on for meditation, a regular time should be the aim. This regularity builds up a contributive factor, a quiet but steady and compelling force. We slip into meditation easier under its custom, and come to feel that without it we are incomplete. In this way the twenty or thirty minutes that we set aside become more than a spiritual discipline and greater than a duty we feel urged to fulfil. It takes its place in our lives as a daily sacrament, tuning in to the rhythm of the world.

Now, after so much thought for our surroundings, what about ourselves? How do we set about meditation? What do we do to begin with? What should be our posture? How ought we to think?

Posture is important in so far as it contributes—as do the things surrounding us—to a calm, untroubled attitude. For this reason we should sit in a comfortable position, so that the muscles do not tire and begin to ache, calling out for attention when our thought should be elsewhere. We are not trying to emulate the endurance of the Tibetan monks who can remain in meditation under the most austere conditions, and neither are we concerned with subjugating the body, like the desert fathers or the saints of the Christian Church. That is entirely another matter and is no part of our present work. Our immediate concern is *meditation*, and it would defeat our object to sit on a bed of nails!

On the other hand, we must not simply slump in an easy chair. If we lounge we are asking to fall asleep. Neither is lying down a good position, for the aim is to be alert. Sitting upright we are more likely to think clearly and maintain a dynamic attitude. Also it permits the free circulation of certain currents and is more in line with our 'upward' orientation.

We must therefore find a position that is comfortable but poised. The lotus position shown below is not a posture that everyone can adopt, but it is an example of the type at which we should aim. It enables the spine to be kept erect and the head rightly balanced without effort; the weight is off the

The Lotus Position

arms, the hands are at rest, and the legs form the base of the posture in a way that keeps the whole body anchored so that, when in the higher stages which the yogis reach, it will still remain steady through its perfect poise.

For those who cannot manage this position, the sitting posture seen in many Egyptian drawings is equally good. Here the back may be supported to keep it erect, the feet are flat on the ground and hands placed loosely on each leg. Again, whatever posture we choose, it will be helpful to adopt it in every meditation that we can. Attitudes make associations in the subconscious; lying down is associated with sleeping, for instance, and kneeling with prayer. Therefore, our meditation posture will assume a special meaning in our unconscious and aid our slipping quickly into the right meditative state.

The first deliberate action when we are settled in place is relaxation. The word 'deliberate' is worth noting here, because from now on each process that we carry out must be an intended and directed act of the will. True meditation is not a negative sitting back in reverie—as said before, but always to be remembered. It is a positive, carefully directed and quite scientific method of working with the consciousness according to spiritual laws.

For anyone wanting to go fully into the subject of relaxation, there are any amount of books on it and methods taught. But for our purpose, a simple and rapid technique of relaxing all the muscles should be enough; we do not want to devote our meditation time to thought on the physical body for any longer than we need.

We must, however, watch against tension creeping up. Concentration is apt to make us frown—if not clench hands and teeth! This makes no contribution to the calm we are seeking and the general pervasion of well-being which meditation should bring. It may even be harmful, bringing stress and fatigue. So a short but deliberate relaxing exercise will make a wise beginning, with a moment of focus on each possible 'culprit', from forehead and eyes, right down to the feet. After a time this will become an automatic and stream-lined proceeding, taking even less than a minute, but to begin with it is worth some care.

Slowing down the rhythm of the breathing also has a relaxing effect. A quiet out-breathing while thinking—and saying aloud if possible—'peace' or any other quietening word with each letting go of tension, will be found a com-bined tranquillising act. The relaxing process is backed up by the rhythm of the breathing and the effect on the subcon-scious of words and sound.

As we gradually quieten and lengthen the breathing, the whole system slows down. Physical relaxing has only been a preliminary, now we have to calm the emotions and the mind. But in line with our aim of achieving serenity, the breathing should never be extended beyond comfort or held in a way to involve strain. The objective is to establish a quiet, slow rhythm that will steady the whole system, giving us freedom to proceed. Extensive breathing exercises should not be undertaken in connection with meditation at this stage. They can hold real danger and beginners should beware of elaborate methods often used in the East. They are not wise for the western aspirant.

But, as with relaxation, we can follow a simple method that will serve to tranquillise physically, emotionally and mentally, and draw in the attention to a rhythmic calm. Counting up to eight or ten quietly with the indrawing of the breath, and again with the outward breathing, helps to establish this, and if this exercise is repeated eight or ten times, it will set afoot the habit of the rhythm and be suffi-cient for our purpose to begin with.

We shall return to the use of the breath at a later stage, in connection with the different meditative processes, but for now, it should slip below the threshold of consciousness, with the physical disciplines we spoke of earlier. These are not our objective now; we have worked with them in the past in one form or another or we would not have reached our present point of wishing to meditate. Their purificatory action will stand us in good stead now, and under no circumstances should that be negated. But we are looking in another direction when we set our foot on the path of meditation and are moving on to subtler practices and demands.

Emotional tranquillity is the next step to achieve, and it may be somewhat harder on account of its close link with thought. Moods of depression, fear, worry, impatience—the possible feelings that can interfere are legion. But we must firmly reject them for the period of the meditation, rising above them and withdrawing the attention from both them and the activities of the day, which will lead us back continually—if we permit them—to the reactions and feelings that are blocking the way.

The emotions will respond, like the physical body, to thoughts of serenity and the rhythm of the quietened breath. If need be, a deliberate minute or two can be spent in calming any persistent attitudes and reactions or recalcitrant moods. A helpful method with this is substitution, for these things will probably lie too deep to be transmuted in a minute or two. Calm may be established by substituting feelings of an opposite nature to those disturbing us, and this may also prove to have quite a redeeming effect. Once we have achieved a measure of this, we are launched on the task of concentration. We have got our feet at last on the ladder that reaches up to the worlds of the mind.

Irrigators guide the water; fletchers straighten arrows;
carpenters bend wood; wise men shape themselves.

The Dhammapada

V · THE FOOT OF THE STAIRWAY

Few have no difficulty in controlling the mind. It is an almost universal problem. But to realize this may help to offset the feelings of defeat and inadequacy so apt to overwhelm us, often building up to a sense of guilt because of our poor efforts and resulting in discouragement, if not in the giving up of the whole affair.

All these reactions only undermine our efforts and weaken the needed positivity of approach, and we shall do better if we raise a sturdy spirit and continue hopefully despite apparent failure. Concentration is, after all, a mental challenge. This should fire the will to succeed, so that tirelessly we renew our efforts, patiently return the mind to the track we set it in, unflaggingly continue until it obeys our will.

The mind is sometimes likened in the East to a monkey, with its tendency to leap continually from branch to branch and follow an endless pattern of activity. This analogy not only illustrates the restlessness of the mind, but the fact that it is a real 'entity' or part of ourselves which has its own identity and its own inclinations, quite apart from the self who is attempting to control it. In fact, it often rebels defiantly against the instructions we may give it, ignoring them entirely and going its own way.

This suggests that in attempting to induce concentration, it will pay us to play the mind with skill rather than bludgeon it into obedience, and so alienate the co-operation it might have otherwise been willing to give. To quote Ernest Wood, who has written and lectured much on the art of controlling the mind:

> In all these matters we must do no violence. We are not hard and lofty masters, whipping a wild animal into sullen obedience. . . . To command the mind is one thing. To teach it as a willing and happy pupil continually finding new delights of experience in healthy functioning is quite another.
>
> *Concentration*

The handling of the mind is a hair-line path. We need the collaboration of its interest and power, we need to set in motion the processes of thought which magically form the medium between the subjective and objective, the abstract mind and the brain. Yet we must exert some discipline; we must emerge the master, for once we come to something like meditation the battle is on and success or failure will depend upon whether or not we are in control.

At every stage of meditation, concentration is the brickwork. Upon it depends the building of the entire edifice. And so, right from the foundation we may as well come to grips with it, knowing it will be needed on every level that we attain.

There are two kinds of concentration; one is spontaneous and automatic, the other deliberate and controlled. Those who believe they have control of the mind because they can happily focus for a long time on something that absorbs them may be surprised and disillusioned when they come to set it to something it has no interest in; this proves to be a very different thing. In spontaneous concentration the mind is really obeying some strong emotional or mental motivation, such as desire, interest, excitement or an impulse of some kind which keeps it engrossed—'spellbound'. In other words, it is concentrating under its own volition or that of the feeling nature. It *wants* to do this, it is its line of least resistance; it is not doing it because it was told.

Deliberate, controlled concentration, on the other hand, is carried out on the orders of the self at the centre, the 'I', and this is entirely another matter. There is probably little emotional urge or desire behind it, and the 'order' may be dull and unattractive to the mind. Therefore it turns away, reluctant to make the effort and runs down the first escape route it can find—for who has not at least a streak of laziness in his mind? But here comes the tussle; we must pull it back and back, for only by training it to accept discipline will it ever become an instrument of use on the higher planes.

The reasons for this take us straight away to the subjective nature of meditation. Abstract and spiritual matters have an intangible quality which makes it genuinely hard for the mind to find something to take hold of, something it can really focus on. There is often no ready point that it can grasp, and if it has not learnt obedience to our directing will, there is little chance of it holding satisfactorily to such an elusive trail. Another reason is that spiritual concepts are often difficult, involving different processes of thought from the usual run; the mind must have a certain responsiveness to direction, therefore, to work in this field with any ease, and a lithe and trained power to collaborate which will make it a controlled as well as sensitive instrument, like a personal radar screen.

Even here, however, we can get a certain amount of aid from the emotional nature through aspiration, dedication and other altruistic motives. And it will pay good dividends to give the mind whatever stimulants are available. Generally speaking, the lower nature has not the enthusiasm for spiritual pursuits that it has for personality action, so we shall need to use skill in action and find some 'carrots' to entice it and induce its help.

All these factors indicate how much we are in the hands of our threefold nature, and not yet the masters of ourselves that we should like to be. As we come up against these lessons, the value of the charioteer symbology comes to mind again and again. We find through hard experience what need there is to keep poised while the reins of the three horses run through our hands, pulling this way and then that, and while, above all, we try to keep hold of the 'winged one' that takes us, on thought, to the ends of the earth in a flash.

Because of all this, most of us will find that some disciplining exercises help to 'tune up' the mind before undertaking meditation. Those with highly trained minds will, of course, not need to do this. Before we go any further, perhaps it should be said, to save ourselves from too much discomfiture, that some types of mind are 'legitimately' worse at concentrating than others. They are more diffuse by nature, so that focus is more difficult and may never be attained to quite the extent that it is by those of a more direct and dynamic type. Yet such minds may be more receptive and able to grasp and interpret subjective concepts better than those with ready focussing power. So we should try to assess our own abilities and see where our weaknesses lie. In this way we can both take courage from our assets and work at whatever we find our deficiencies to be.

For example, those who tend to be vague, dreamy and abstracted will need to develop their minds along objective lines, while those who are over-objective and tend to be practical and precise will need to cultivate more subjective attitudes, imagination and ability to think abstractly and in universal terms.

A simple exercise for those in the first category is to look for a minute at something like a picture, a building, a shop window, and then write down the details observed. This must be done precisely and the result checked, and although it may sound more appropriate for the kindergarten than for preparing to meditate, it is of specific value in developing ability to focus attention without the help of interest. It trains the mind to concentrate *to order*, and this is a most important and valuable step; it is a necessary initial stage before the more difficult matter of concentrating on subjects that are abstract and abstruse.

Another exercise of this nature, and one that would also be useful for the practical type of mind, is to evoke a picture of something that is familiar, and hold it steadily in the mind's eye, building it carefully in every detail for a predetermined length of time. In this we are evoking the power to visualize as well as concentrate and recall, and may well come up against the vagaries of the imagination, which is apt to play all kinds of tricks. For this reason we must again check the picture we have built. The particular value of this exercise— which, like the previous one, may seem exceedingly simple —is that, added to this training in concentration, it reveals the capricious nature of the mind; it may give us a salutary lesson on the watch that we must keep on it when we send it on longer and higher flights.

Collaborating with the imagination is one of the mind's favourite tricks. It uses it for all sorts of purposes: to escape from the dullness of the task it has been set, to cover up its inadequacies, to build the concepts in which it delights. In all kinds of ways the imagination is a ready partner, aiding and abetting the volatile mind. Yet in its creativity, the imagination is one of our most valuable instruments, and a necessary factor in several phases of the meditation process, as we shall see when we come to examine these.

Imagination is both reproductive and creative, and it can function at several levels. It links with sensation, feeling, thinking and also intuition. It will be obvious, therefore, how important it is to understand this function and be able to recognize and control it and use it when we have need. Some people, of course, have more imagination than others, but whether it is a matter of needing to cultivate it or of having too much, exercises in which it is deliberately evoked, used, and then dismissed are a valuable preliminary training. They will teach us to handle the imagination, to use it creatively instead of it running away with us, and will also make us aware of its nature and extent.

Visualization is a good starting point for training creative imagination. A symbol may be visualized and then deliberately extended. For instance, a triangle may be pictured and then the lines extended to form a diamond; this can then be deepened into three dimensions and the many facets of a diamond and its scintillation added. A circle can, in the same way, be extended into a star, alternatively, we can visualize a number, and then add others to it one by one, until a row of them is held clearly in the picture.

An elaboration of this exercise is to build up in the mind's eye a picture on a wall, or a scene in the countryside. This could follow these lines:

Exercise in training the Imagination

Imagine a quiet corner on a summer's day.

Permit 3 or 4 minutes to build up the picture of it in a garden, in the country, or by the sea.

Mentally sketch in every detail, filling in the colours and seeing everything that makes the environment complete.

Now step into the place that has been built; imagine the

warmth and light of the sun, the sound it is filled with
and the scent on the air.

Enjoy these for a minute, always maintaining the position
of the observer.

Then deliberately withdraw and dismiss the picture—not
just when tired of it, but after, say, two minutes, or
whatever time has been decided upon.

This type of exercise can also be used to imagine a situation which we have to face: we see ourselves meeting all its exigencies and problems and satisfactorily getting through whatever is entailed. This has been proved in psychiatry to be a valuable technique for eliminating fear and anxious anticipation; it is a definite method of replacing negativity with a positive attitude and of using the imagination for constructive ends.

Whatever kind of exercise we choose, *we* must select it, not the imagination. We should choose something either constructive and conducive to serene or positive thought, or else neutral and not disturbing in any way. The time factor also should be decided before beginning as this, again, marks the measure of our control.

The essence of all these exercises lies in our not being carried away by the imagination. We deliberately set it to build whatever we choose and infuse it with living quality, then we bring the exercise to a close. The whole process is kept under our command and we never lose the consciousness that we are the *observer* and in control. We give the mind 'rope', as it were, to have a game with fancy, but we use the game ourselves to watch it in action and practise handling it according to our will.

Mention has frequently been made of the will, and although we cannot go far into this deep and important subject here, it is a factor that must be recognized in any approach to meditation. We need it first of all to make room in time and space before our meditating can begin—as we saw all too well in the previous chapter. Then we need it to maintain the daily rhythm, and we need it, above all, to concentrate—which means at every stage on the way.

The will is something most people know little about, beyond perhaps having registered that they have too little or too much. In fact, it is difficult to understand what the will is and it is apt to be confused with self-will and forceful expression of intention. It has an unfortunate connection with the word 'willful', but it is not, as so many believe, simply fixed determination or one-pointed drive. Neither is it self-will in the usual meaning of the word.

The will has been called the divine aspect in man which puts him in rapport with the essence of existence, with the purpose synthesizing all life. It is certainly an intrinsic part of his being. 'Men are wills', wrote St Augustine, and Assagioli calls the will 'the function which is most directly related to the self.' He describes the following six stages of the 'voluntary action' in his book *Psychosynthesis*, explaining that 'the will is not only and simply *will power* according to the usual conception' and that all these stages or phases are necessary for its complete and effective expression:

1. Purpose—Goal;
2. Deliberation and motivation based on values;
3. Choice—Decision;
4. Affirmation—Command;
5. Planning;
6. Direction of the execution of the plan.

Recognition of the function of the will in all these different ways will clarify its constitution and position. It will also be obvious that all of the above stages are closely concerned with the process of meditation. We might even say, when we bear in mind that the will is at the core of all concentration, that the success of our meditating will eventually depend as much upon our skilful use of the will as anything else.

As with all the other aspects of our threefold nature, it comes back to the self at the centre to see that the will is rightly used. It is a function of the self that can be used for any purpose, and its right development is a highly important factor. The will-to-good is one of the greatest spiritual forces. To realize this and train the will to provide a rightly motivating impulse is one of the most valuable steps of our 'inner education'.

Like imagination, we may lack will or have too much, but in either case it will serve the same purpose to carry out some exercises that will develop its control. These, as in the case of telling the mind to concentrate without the aid of interest, should consist of things that, in the specific sense, we have no desire to do, otherwise they will not cultivate the will. They can be definite, planned exercises, or small daily tasks, like the keeping of certain rhythms or fulfilling of resolves. There are a hundred ways throughout the day in which we can train the will to be our henchman, and again, as with concentration and imagination, it can often be done as if it were a game. The 'ludic instinct', or drive to play, has been found to provide a valuable psychological incentive in training and developing the various aspects of ourselves.

The aim of all these different exercises in concentration, imagination and the will is the same. They teach the co-ordination individually of physical body, emotions, mind, and the integration of these three, with the will, into a unified whole. They also help to assert the position of the 'I' at the centre, the observer, director, self. And all this is valuable preparation for the higher building in meditation which we intend to attempt now.

In her book *From Intellect to Intuition* Alice Bailey writes that two things aid this preliminary work of co-ordination:

First the endeavour to gain control of the mind, through the endeavour to live a concentrated life. The life of consecration and dedication, which is so distinctive of the mystic, gives place to the life of concentration and meditation—distinctive of the knower. The organization of the thought life . . . and, secondly, the practice of concentration, regularly, every day at some set time if possible, make for the one-pointed attitude, and these two together spell success.   (*p. 206*)

This brings us back to the mind, our specific instrument in meditation. Mind control has always been a first requirement in all intellectual mysticism. St Dionysius wrote that three things were required to attain to higher and truer vision:

The first is, possession of one's mind. The second is, a mind that is free. The third is, a mind that can see. How can we acquire this speculative mind? By a habit of mental concentration.

FRANZ PFEIFFER
Meister Eckhart

Eastern methods make the same demand. There must be control of the mental apparatus and often extreme measures are taken to develop it. This is illustrated in the following amusing story recounted by Alexandra David-Neel. A method of ascertaining the degree of concentration sometimes used with novices in Tibet is to place a small, burning lamp on the head. These lamps are filled with butter and will last a considerable time, but will fall off with the slightest movement. In this particular case, runs the story, a lama who was trying to train a pupil to concentrate, set a lamp on the young man's head. The novice commendably kept it in place all through the night and only set it down when the butter was burnt out. But he had mistaken the aim of the exercise, thinking it was to ensure that he did not move. The next day the lama came and questioned why the lamp was on the ground, and the pupil explained that it had burnt out during the night. But the lama sternly retorted—'How could you know that the lamp went out or even that you had a lamp on your head, if you had reached true concentration of mind?' We can hardly expect to reach such standards!

'The mind wavers, Krishna,' cries Arjuna, the disciple, in the scriptural story of the *Bhagavad Gita*. 'Turbulent, impetuous, forceful, I think it is as hard to hold as the wind!' And the Master replies:

> Without doubt, mighty armed one, the wavering mind is hard to hold; but through assiduous practice . . . it may be held firm. For him whose mind is uncontrolled, union is hard to obtain . . . but for him whose mind has been brought under his sway, who is controlled, it may be won.
>
> *Book VI*

Far from being a dull and formidable obstacle, concentration or control of the mind begins to appear, as we proceed, like a magical opening of a door. Upon it we find depends not only achieving the higher reaches of the mind, but the down to earth facility with which we conduct our lives. It reaches into the depths of every action and qualifies our thinking from morning until night. As Keyserling wrote in *The Travel Diary of a Philosopher*:

> Undoubtedly the power of concentration is the real propelling power of the whole psychic mechanism. Nothing heightens our capacity for performance as much as its increase; every success, no matter in what domain, can be traced back to the intelligent exploitation of this power.

Alice Bailey in the book just mentioned also points out the relationship of concentration in the spheres of the outer and inner life:

> True concentration grows out of a concentrated,
> thought-governed life, and the first step for the
> aspirant is to begin to organize his daily life, regulate
> his activities and become focussed and one-pointed in
> his manner of living. This is possible to all who care
> enough to make the needed effort. . . . This is the first
> and basic essential.
>
> *p. 207*

The word 'concentration', coming from the Latin, means 'bringing together', or 'drawing to a common central point'. Patanjali, the Hindu teacher of many centuries before Christ, defined it in this way:

> The binding of the perceiving consciousness to a certain
> region is attention or concentration.

He also gave the encouragement that 'Sustained concentration is meditation'. Alice Bailey elaborates this in *The Light of the Soul*:

> Meditation is but the extension of concentration and
> grows out of the facility a man achieves in 'fixing the
> mind' at will on any particular object. It falls under
> the same rules and conditions as concentration and the
> only distinction between the two is the *time* element.
> Having achieved the capacity to focus the mind
> steadily upon an object, the next step is developing the
> power to hold the mind stuff or chitta★ unwaveringly

★ The word *chitta* is used in the East for the faculty of thought, mental substance and the sum total of the mental processes.

occupied with that object or thought for a prolonged period.

p. 247

In the same book, seven stages of concentration are mentioned and these, briefly are:

1. The choice of some object upon which to concentrate.
2. The withdrawing of the mind from the periphery to the centre, so that the avenues of outer perception and contact are stilled (the senses), and the consciousness is no longer outgoing.
3. The centring of the consciousness in the head.
4. The application of the mind to the object chosen.
5. Visualization of the object.
6. Extension of the specific mental concepts that have formed to more general and universal concepts.
7. An attempt to arrive at that which lies back of the form.

If we can do all this, we are already launched upon the enterprise of meditation. There will only remain the matter of right choice of theme and objective, and also adequate patience and persistence. These will be key qualities needed for the work that lies ahead, for no matter what kind of mind we have, we are approaching new country, and shall need to persuade it patiently to pursue our objective there. But the least of us need not be afraid to venture towards these realms, the key to success lies in constant effort far more than intellectual prowess. In fact, like the hare and the tortoise, the slower mind will often keep to the course with more persistence. The sporadic efforts apt to be made in a field of this extension can even be detrimental, for they cause a continual sense of failure.

Steady perseverance, on the other hand, sets afoot the

power of habit and a spiritual exercise carried out with rhythm is like a rolling snowball. It gathers to itself through the effect of its own continual action. A few minutes' concentration, carried out every day, will produce far better results than much longer periods which are only intermittent and have no rhythm backing them up. This has been said more than once, but it is worth remembering. Patience and persistence should be our most cared-for tools.

We are starting on a long journey, the high adventure of finding our own Souls, and having wandered for eons from our birth-place, we must be prepared for some initial testings and delays. It is bound to take some effort at the beginning to get under way. Adjustments will be needed, obstacles will appear and diversions may attract us down unwonted lanes. We shall find we are called upon to demonstrate our earnestness and intention over and over again. But it is said that this is the testing through which we affirm our right to penetrate the places of the Soul. And undoubtedly, we cannot expect to walk there until we have proved ourselves and are known.

So, this is a point of high promise, difficulties or not, and we are standing at one of the most joyous moments of our lives. The lonely, fragmentary consciousness of the human frame is seeing its way towards the Soul, the Self, the Whole from which it came, and is set, like an aircraft turning on to the take-off runway, to begin the flight that will lift it into the sun.

If we think that our nature is limited by the little wave of our being which is our conscious waking self, we are ignorant of our true being. The relation of our life to a larger spiritual world betrays itself even in the waking consciousness through our intellectual ideals, our moral aspirations, our cravings for beauty, and our longing for perfection. Behind our conscious self is our secret being without which the superficial consciousness cannot exist or act. Consciousness in us is partly manifest and partly hidden. We can enlarge the waking part of it by bringing into play ranges of our being which are now hidden. It is our duty to become aware of ourselves as spiritual beings, instead of falsely identifying ourselves with the body, life or mind.

RADHAKRISHNAN
Eastern Religions and Western Thought

VI · TOPOGRAPHY AND TECHNIQUES

It is high time now to consider the field of meditation. Having made our preparations for the venture, what about the territory we propose to explore? Meditation has been compared to sending a missile into outer space, and the analogy is helpful and remarkably exact. We are literally shooting off from our earthbound situation when we direct the consciousness upwards in meditation. Like a satellite leaving the launching pad, we are probing out to areas not yet sign-posted, to regions far beyond those that are known. There are all the potentialities of a flight in outer space, for a true meditation should closely approximate the procedure of a missile—careful preparation and alignment, take-off or ascendence, orbit and return to earth.

Therefore we need to have some knowledge, so far as it is possible, of the area to be traversed, the conditions we may expect to meet and the fine attunements and 'technicalities' that may be involved in the flight. In other words, we need to make ourselves familiar with the laws of its 'dynamics', for in meditation we are definitely dealing with the action of forces in a subtle energy field. It is a process following laws of vibration and attunement, and as truly a science of 'inner space' as is astrophysics of the outer cosmic realm. This analogy, in fact, gives a good idea of the great potentialities of the Science of Meditation.

In line with all scientific procedure, it is a deliberate, controlled, step by step process. It is not mystical flight with no rhyme or reason. It is a method of progressing in consciousness through various states or stages, and while the word 'stages' indicates the essential *evolving* factor, the word 'states' suggests two aspects of the spheres of meditation. It contributes the idea of 'states' or conditions of consciousness and also 'states' in the sense of territory—of areas into which we move—and both of these meanings have significance.

Perhaps the best way of explaining this and approaching the topography of the inner regions is through the diagram given here of the 'planes' of the solar system. This chart of the differentiations of life-consciousness-energy is widely used in study of the esoteric, or inner, evolution of the consciousness of man. It indicates the sevenfold energy field, or seven planes of manifestation, which range from dense to abstract levels like steps on a giant stairway, and although this concept may at first over-simplify, it gives us a blueprint with which to work.

Each of the seven planes of the energy field of the solar system is shown here to have seven differentiations or sub-planes, which correspond in quality to the greater seven to which they belong. The higher reaches hardly concern us, they are too far beyond even our imagining to be usefully considered at this point. But to keep the over-all sweep in mind, so far as we are able to, will ensure some sense of the gigantic proportions of the way on which we are embarked.

The septenary structure appears in many fields. Seven notes make up the octave, seven colours form the spectrum. Seven streams of energy are recognized as universal and giving rise to seven psychological types. And did not the

THE PLANES OF BEING

I		
II		ABSTRACT LEVELS OF WHICH WE KNOW LITTLE
III		
IV INTUITIONAL OR BUDDHIC		
V MENTAL OR MANASIC PLANE	△ SOUL ○ MENTAL UNIT	
VI EMOTIONAL OR ASTRAL PLANE		PERSONALITY
VII PHYSICAL PLANE		FIRST ETHER SECOND ETHER THIRD ETHER FOURTH ETHER GASEOUS OR MENTAL LIQUID OR EMOTIONAL DENSE OR PHYSICAL

author of Genesis ascribe seven partitions of time to the decrees of the Creator, that man should be able to number his days? The seven Spirits before the throne of God, whom St John proclaimed, are reflected in a great many ways and science has yet to explain the meaning of this sevenfold manner of manifestation.

We should not, however, consider this structure as too well defined, that is, with hard and fast dividing lines between the planes and sub-planes. Each of them is characterized by its own range of consciousness, but they also interpenetrate and interact. Each plane, A. A. Bailey tells us, 'is a vast sphere of matter interacting with that above and that below'. We get an idea of this merging of one state into another in the break-down of division between colours and also between tone and tone in the musical scale; overtones emerge, a-tonal qualities, their subtleties becoming more obvious now to the modern ear. So, at the same time as recognizing these graded degrees of estate, we should bear in mind the fine points of relationship and interpenetration.

The concept of 'planes' is also limiting if we take it as meaning 'horizontal'. The planes are spheres of consciousness in which we live—moving, thinking, being in their depth and expansion. Each plane is literally a world of awareness, a world into which we move when we have developed in ourselves its particular quality or vibration. And here is their connection with meditation. The concentrated effort to direct our thinking upwards into more rarefied atmospheres raises our own vibration, attuning us to the higher airs. This brings about the finer sensitivity needed to participate there.

Another way in which this expanding concept might be thought of is suggested in the diagram on p. 88, the central circle indicating the extent of physical plane consciousness and each curve marking the progressive areas we attain. But since we are dealing with abstract concepts, with realities it is impossible to define, any two-dimensional diagrams of this nature can only suggest in a totally inadequate way the different strata or aspects of our planetary domain.

To come to our present purpose of examining the regions we live in and those to which we aspire, we are really only concerned with the three lowest or 'densest' planes, the physical, emotional and mental. The average man is fully conscious only on the physical level we are told; he almost encompasses the seven stages of the emotional region, but is only developing his consciousness of the lowest areas of the mental plane.

This may be surprising, yet when we think of the vast sweep of this mental region, of the difference that lies between primitive, palaeolithic man and the average modern scientist, we get an idea of the immense expanse that we are considering. From dense, unthinking, automatic mental reaction, motivated only by physical or emotional drives, man has slowly awakened and learned to use his mind. We can trace this growth in the pages of history and see how he began to think, how the mind, exerting itself this way and that, gradually became more agile, increasing its ability, extending its reach.

Attainment of each of the sub-planes of the mental plane brings a new world to the expanding consciousness. It could be compared with the ever wider vistas that meet us when we scale a mountain side, arriving continually at higher vantage points, with the horizon pushed back and new worlds at our feet. So the growing mind encompasses what was previously beyond its range, and our magical power to think paves more and more of the pathway that will take us eventually to the lands the gods have reached.

To understand the different ranges of this mental region more fully, because this is the area we are most concerned with in meditation to begin with, imagine being at the lowest step of the mental stairway. Our thinking would be slow and confined to facts of immediate concern; we should have no interest outside the things of the physical world, and little power to relate or plan or look beyond the moment.

Nowadays this is hard to imagine, for little thinking is confined entirely to the physical level; some emotional influence is bound to creep in and colour the simplest thought. In this way the next field of sensitive perception begins to open out; we move into a further strata of consciousness, thinking in terms of feeling, preferences, relationships, and developing more awareness as the mind probes slowly out. Yet still no active mental power exerts itself; thinking is simply impulsive, motivated by feeling and limited to meeting the immediate external needs and desires.

But action breeds action; gradually we become more mentally vigorous, able to cover a wider field, to think out, plan, conjecture, relate and perceive. The mind becomes an ally dedicated to our achievement until, like a mountain goat, we are able to leap from point to point in the thought area surrounding us, scaling our problems and discovering new fields.

So we become masters of the three lower levels of the mental plane. The average human being encompasses only these, but in the diagram on p. 75 the 'mental unit' will be seen indicated on the fourth sub-plane. This we may take as the unfolding point of mental energy, the inheritance due to be taken up, and through it we shall eventually make the fourth sub-plane our habitat. From here we shall look up to the subtler sub-planes, quickening our vibration and refining our thinking, that we may contact abstract worlds as yet beyond imagining and grasp the 'life' of the next dimension consciously and rightfully.

Lest we become impatient, it is wise to remember here that each of these stages takes a great while to achieve. Palaeontologists say we have been some half million years reaching our present level of thinking, and esoteric teachings speak of the dawn of human consciousness taking place millions of years ago. So we cannot expect to leap the next steps as quickly as we might like to. It is a gradual process, not a sudden transformation. Also, although we have used the words 'planes' and 'strata', it must always be remembered that they are areas of consciousness with no dividing lines between them to be crossed like the Rubicon, with triumph at the achievement. They are fields of force in which we gradually make our way as we increase our thought capacity and raise our mental quality in their subtler, freer airs.

This may be better understood if we think of it in terms of vibration. It is said that the higher we go on every plane, the higher the atomic vibratory rate. This not only seems to be logical, but is borne out by our experience on the lower planes. There is a very different 'feel' on the different levels of thinking. Thought on material, routine matters, the drab affairs of every day, keeps us labouring, heavily enveloped, on their horizontal plane. On the other hand, thought directed vertically, whether to spiritual subjects or ideas or ideals of any kind, has a spontaneous lifting effect. It inspires with the higher quality contacted, and we often feel the stimulation of this higher vibration mentally and emotionally and even physically as well.

Since abstract thought is therefore of a higher vibratory rate than the thinking of the 'concrete mind' on material and objective levels, it is obvious that we shall need to raise the vibration of our own mental substance in order to 'connect' intelligently in the subtler realms. And meditation is, of course, the golden method of achieving this, training the thinking, as it does, to approach and become acclimatized to these spheres.

But meditation is not the only means, and all activity which raises thought to abstract concepts aids this elevating process. For instance, higher mathematics and many kinds of scientific calculation are carried out on these high levels beyond the fringes of concrete knowledge, and those who work in these fields become 'at home' in areas which are super-normal for most of us. Such work could, in fact, be called meditation. So, too, could the search for inspiration by the poet, the artist, the musician, and the attunement with higher worlds which works of genius reveal.

It is well known that consciousness of the lower self is forgotten when focus is really established on such levels; the personality is absorbed into timelessness in the effort to catch and frame and bring into objectivity the concepts concerned. Stories illustrating this are found in the lives of all the great composers, authors, poets, artists, and scientists are proverbially 'absent-minded'.

Perhaps one of the most outstanding examples of this is the story told of Socrates, who one day was seen to be standing in the market place, thinking about something he could not resolve from dawn until mid-day. By that time people were beginning to gather round, watching to see how long he would continue wrapt in thought in this way. But he continued without apparently noticing them until dusk and on into the night. People, by now, were bringing out their beds into the street in order to see when he finally 'came back to earth', and at last, at dawn, he offered up a prayer and went away. Perhaps this was a case of illumination rather than pursuit of a concept on a higher plane. We cannot know, but it illustrates the state that can be attained of complete unawareness of all that is 'lower', or of the physical world.

There are many things that entice the mind to soar above its usual levels—divine enticements like beauty, grandeur and perfection in all kinds of form. The higher spheres offer many magnetic revelations and we should give them 'head room', for they offer a pulling power—like the hand of God stretched out—which will help us to step out onto the uplands of our being. If they do not appear readily about us, then let us search for them; they can be great salvaging factors which expedite our spiritual way.

At this point it might be good to define what is meant by 'spiritual'. Do we confine it to 'religion'? Is it 'to do with the Soul'? An interesting definition is given by the Tibetan writer Djwhal Khul:

Everything is spiritual which tends towards understanding, towards kindness, towards that which is productive of beauty and which can lead man on to a fuller expression of his divine potentialities.

He also writes:

The word 'spiritual' covers every phase of living experience. . . . That is spiritual which lies beyond the present point of achievement; it is that which embodies the vision and urges the man on towards a goal higher than the one attained.

This means that every next step can be a spiritual opportunity, that no matter where we stand on the ladder of evolution, that is spiritual which is our next point of achievement. This is an inspiring encouragement, something to take hold of with the heart and the mind, and it gives a great perspective for the ordering of our lives.

Although all means of penetrating into the regions of the unmanifested teach the mind to function in those spheres, meditation is a means that will greatly expedite the raising of our vibration that we may be genuine citizens there.

It will be obvious that each step in this process has to be consolidated. Flights that lift but spearhead actual achievement, and the high point gained has to be built in and stabilized. It is here that the habit of daily meditation plays such a valuable part, and this is why transmutation of the threefold lower nature has been so stressed in spiritual teachings.

Dense, untransmuted substance obstructs the higher degrees of communion, and here the purification wrought throughout the centuries by religious disciplines repays a hundredfold. The steady building in of higher qualities permits connection with the world of the Soul through development of its qualities. It might be compared to building up a deposit account in the bank in our favour; we store in to our substance a balance that will tell. And once it is established we shall never go bankrupt; we shall have behind us 'credit' that is sound.

All this gives meaning to the *process* of meditation, and particularly to its preliminary stages—alignment, dedication and attunement. These are all methods of bringing the lower, brain consciousness into that state of 'refinement' or adjustment and elevation which will permit of contact with the Soul. Meditation, too, requires a certain amount of resolve and so brings in intention, which is perhaps our most needed propelling power.

The meaning of the word 'alignment' will be abundantly clear. We are taught that the Soul, as a 'centre' of spiritual energy, has its habitat above the plane of the mental unit (see diagram on p 75). Our aim, as is the aim of the whole evolution of man in the 'three worlds', is alignment of the threefold personality with the higher Self or Soul. Our task is, therefore, to make a fourfold alignment. But this will come eventually. To begin with, the three lower bodies are our primary concern. Only when they provide a balanced, smoothly integrated vehicle shall we be able to begin to bridge the next gap and make our alignment with the Soul. True abstract thought only becomes possible when the personality has achieved a reciprocal vibration to that of the Soul and is therefore sufficiently aligned to form a moderately unimpeded channel. Then the great leaders of mankind emerge, the inspired writers bring down their vision and the higher synthetic thinkers give their concepts to the world.

This alignment is sometimes attained in moments of supreme endeavour, at times of stress, intense aspiration, even in times of physical danger. We have probably all experienced moments when crisis faced us and we felt we had a supreme strength, the mind worked like lightning and we know instinctively what to do. We 'rose' to the occasion as it is said. This may occur but rarely, yet we do not forget that we felt no fear in those moments, had no doubts, were fully able to meet the demands, and it gives us confidence that such alignment is possible and illustrates the high point to be consciously attained.

The following *Technique for achieving Alignment* indicates the various stages of the process and can be used as a preparation in every meditation that we undertake. Gradually the stages will be streamlined as we become used to them, so that the exercise need only take a minute or two in the end. But to begin with, it should be gone into slowly and carefully, for the preliminaries make the sure foundation from which the edifice of our meditation will rise up.

Technique for achieving Alignment

The physical body is the house of our feelings and reactions, and with the brain cells we carry out the activity of the mind. The quiet co-operation of the physical body is therefore a first essential when we start to meditate. Right poise and relaxation help to bring this about, as mentioned in Chapter IV, and the following is a simple way to proceed:

1. Having found a comfortable position, make a deliberate effort to relax all physical tension. Think right through the body from head to foot, relaxing each part. Nervous tension must be consciously released, and after a minute or two we should be still physically poised, but *at rest*.

This is important because any muscles held tense will begin to ache and fidget as time goes on and this will draw back our attention. We need to forget the physical body to pursue our higher intention, so we must see that it is put at ease.

2. The breathing should now be quietened and slowed down. Counting, say five, six, seven, or whatever proves a comfortable rate, while drawing in the breath and again with its exhalation helps to create a rhythm, which has its own quietening effect. Find a count which steadies down the breathing but does not stretch the capacity, or it will be difficult to maintain it and, again, the objective is to establish a quiet *ease*. Newcomers to meditation should never attempt elaborate breathing exercises. They can seriously over-stimulate, which only mitigates against the need for us to become gradually and steadily aligned and attuned.

Once the rhythm is established, stop counting, or it can become a mental habit difficult to break. The breathing must be forgotten once the rhythm is set afoot. A good way of doing this is to use a phrase with the same number of syllables as the count, and if we use appropriate words, this takes us smoothly on to the next stage. For example, if we have been mentally counting six on each in and out breath, the following phrase, again said silently, will be in the same rhythm and at the same time establish the next stage:

'I am at ease and all my feelings are serene.'

Any words can be used which embody the stage or quality to be next attained, but no word or phrase should be repeated more than a few times, as if it is continued it may have a hypnotic effect and this is *not* the objective of meditation.

3. Polarization is now on the emotional level. Draw in

the consciousness from all reactions and attitudes, drop all antipathies and anticipations, and try to stand in consciousness at a still, central point. This may be helped, again, by framing in words the state being aimed at, saying for example:

'I am a centre of calm, clarity and light.'

Visualization can also help in creating this still centre of consciousness. The emotional body can be imagined and visualized as a smooth and limpid pool, with a quiet, reflective quality which will offer no impediment to alignment with the mind.

If strong emotions are playing in us which make this difficult—a recently aroused anger, for instance, or excitement or high feeling of any kind, a short technique using the symbology of water, which is the symbol of the emotions, can be very helpful. Visualize a stormy sea, with the waves running high, depicting and expressing the strong or turbulent emotion. See this emotion expending itself as the energy in the waves while you visualize them sweeping by and breaking. Then see the whole picture gradually quietening; calm down your sea deliberately until it stretches out to the horizon with only a ripple here and there to show its living responsiveness to the sunlight streaming down.

4. Now raise the consciousness to the mind. Here again the attention must be drawn in from the periphery and from all extraneous thoughts to the centre. This central point of focus will be held steady by thought on a particular theme, and this will be gone into in Chapter VII. For our present purpose of alignment, a simple phrase like the following can be used:

'I am a point of focussed thought.'

Have confidence that you now stand as a clear channel,
stilled, lighted and prepared to communicate with the
Soul, to direct the lower threefold attention, like the
beam of a searchlight, towards the area in which that
Being dwells.

Three parts of the fourfold alignment have now been
achieved. The fourth part is our next—and main—concern.

Dedication now comes into the picture. As an attitude, it
is currently somewhat out of fashion, but it holds a very
definite propulsive power and should be included at the
beginning of every meditation. It is both an emotional and
mental activity, in fact, it is a combined use of the aligned
threefold nature—brain cells, feeling and thought all being
required. It gathers up this triple energy and directs it in the
way we wish it to be used, thus setting afoot both an orien-
tating and a propulsive power.

But there is more to the technique of dedication than may
at first appear. The act of dedicating ourselves to a specific
objective clarifies the intention and, ensures that the meditation has a recognized purpose and an acknowledged goal to
which we aspire. Then the assertion of our aspiration not
only focusses the personality forces, but brings in the will.
This is an important factor, as we saw when considering
concentration. Without it we should get continually side-
tracked—in fact we might never even begin! And in the
'airy' fields of the more abstract levels its holding and directing power is essential. Dedication is the arrow of the intention.

Dedication has also a subtler and more lasting effect. It is
an act of 'lifting up'. Our forces, after being gathered, are
projected towards the chosen goal, and this aids in the process
of raising the vibration. In religious terms it has 'redeeming'

power, and this is its inner, or occult, effect, brought about by law.

Aspiration, which must be present to a certain extent for all meditation, is the heart—literally—of all dedication. It is the urge, deep-seated in the heart, to reach the goal we see or sense, to serve the high purpose we have chosen. 'Fiery aspiration' is the first means of union with the Soul taught by Patanjali, and Alice Bailey, in her commentary on the Sutras of that great Teacher, writes:

> It is well to point out here that this quality of 'going forth' towards the idea or of straining towards the objective must be so profound in the aspirant that no difficulties can turn him back. . . . Fiery effort, steady persistent longing and enduring faithfulness to an ideal visioned are the *sine qua non* of discipleship. These characteristics must be found in all three bodies, leading to the constant disciplining of the physical vehicle, the steady orientation of the emotional nature and the mental attitude which enables a man to 'count all things but loss' if he can only arrive at his goal.
>
> *The Light of the Soul*, pp. 189–90

This takes the attitude of dedication right into our lives, but as a stage in each meditation, the assertion of these qualities and affirmation of the higher intention bring to bear a projective power which opens up a channel towards the objective. It is a valuable technique for achieving rapport with the realms we seek.

Any simple form can frame our dedication, and we may make it to the Soul, to God, or the universal Creator, to the service of mankind, or to whatever may be our immediate goal. But whatever we choose, let us make use of this power each time we start to meditate. It will add wings to our alignment and firmness to our step.

But above and beyond that, it will relate us to a purpose greater than our own. And this there must always be—a recognition and affirmation of the magnetic thread that draws us on, or we shall achieve little more than temporary and personal satisfaction.

Among the undertakings of the Tibetan initiate when he takes the Bodhisattva vow is that he will remain 'without entering *Nirvana* (bliss) so long as a single blade of grass remains unenlightened'. This supreme vow of at-one-ment and sacrifice may as yet be far outside our humble sphere, but each fragmentary act of dedication that we make is a tiny note in the great orchestral 'sound' which is lifting all life on our planet and taking it towards its eventual goal.

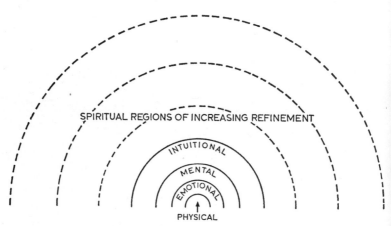

Expanding Consciousness

Dimly the one who seeks hears the faint whisper
    of the Life of God. . . .
Listening is the seed of obedience,
    O Chela on the Path.

An ancient eastern Scripture

VII · THE POOL OF REFLECTION

Meditation is like a jewel of many facets and at this point it would be wise to examine the difference between a few of the aspects of this many-splendoured thing. Then we shall be in a position to decide which to follow, which we need to work at to use effectively and which will be most suitable for any particular purpose.

In view of the current interest in transcendental meditation and eastern schools of various types, it must be said straight-away that the facets of the jewel which we are considering here are those of a positive and creative nature, suitable for the western beginner. The more abstract types of meditation which are practised widely in the East are not always advis-able for those with no previous training, or without reliable guidance. Our western civilization hardly offers the best environment to attempt to practise them anyway.

The mode of the East has produced very different physical bodies, brain cells, attitudes and philosophies from those of the West, and often the imposition of eastern methods of meditation—unless under careful supervision—may have dis-rupting and even harmful effects on those with no experience.

It has been said that the Orient is to the human race what the heart is to the physical body—the source of life or 'inner' vitality; while the Occident corresponds to the brain and mental activity and provides the organizing factor. Be that as it may, each has much to give to each. Oriental thinking has for countless ages bred the ascetic and the meditator and the devotee of the inner, abstract, subjective life. These elements are now fast attracting many followers in the West, who have objectivity and organized minds with which to utilize the teaching. But the marriage must not be too hasty or there may be disharmony. A period of betrothal and assimilation of each other—of tentative experiment and examination—is a wise preliminary to its consummation.

The types of meditation we shall examine now are in the nature of such preliminaries. They are the broad, basic steps of the silent path, the classic stages to be mastered. Briefly, they can be defined as:

Reflective Meditation, which is a strictly mental process, involving thinking on or about a definite subject, theme, word or thought. This is perhaps the simplest form of meditation and the best to start with because it entails the ordinary active although controlled thinking to which the mind is accustomed.

Receptive Meditation, which, as the term suggests, is a holding of the mind still and alert to receive light on a subject, to catch an inspiration or grasp a new realization. It should not be thought of as a negative form of meditation, but might be compared to listening for something which is far away, and which, therefore, demands the mustering of all the attention.

Creative Meditation, which aims at building in thought substance the 'forms' or patterns or channels through which ideas, ideals, energies and qualities can find expression. This, as again the name indicates, is an entirely constructive form of meditation, in which, for example, a 'thought-form' may be built of some needed ideal or quality. This is then strengthened through the energy of our thought, and that thought is an energy—a tangible factor—is becoming widely recognized today. In this way, creative meditation can co-operate with and contribute vitality to such concepts as peace, right relationship, compassion. We will go further into it later, but this is one of the most reconstructive elements of the modern concept of meditation, for through it we can reconstitute both ourselves and our environment and can effectively give aid to humanity and the world where otherwise our services might be of little avail.

Invocation and Prayer are yet another kind of meditation, in which help is asked for, something higher or greater appealed to, forces that are needed called upon. Invocation and prayer are two different forms of making this appeal and we will look at their somewhat different techniques in the next chapter.

As with all matters of the inner worlds, however, there are few definite dividing lines, and the four types of meditation described here all involve something of each other. A creative meditation, in fact, may well include some aspects of all four, as will be seen in the outline given later. So it is as well to practise and become at home with each type, particularly those found more difficult. In this way we become well rounded-out in our meditative abilities and shall be able to build effective channels for the inner work we seek to do.

So, first, we come to the *pool of reflection*. Let us be clear right from the start that a static or negative attitude is not inferred by this phrase. A truly reflective pool has a positive quality of reception and a clarity that enables that above it to be captured.

Having taken up our position and followed all the procedures spoken of in the previous chapters which have prepared for this moment—have prescribed the time and place, put us at ease, aligned us with the inner world we are seeking to work in—we now enter its atmosphere. The subject for reflection will have been chosen before we began. Let us suppose it is a quality like *Serenity*. We repeat the word and begin to consider its meaning, value, significance, and what it is able to bring about.

The first precept is to watch the thinking processes, to keep a check on them, noticing immediately the mind begins to wander, watching if it follows certain lines of association, or gets back to the same grooves again and again. Patiently we must bring it back to the central theme, and here we might take courage from the writer Sri Krishna Prem:

> For countless ages the mind has been turned outwards and has been given a free rein to attach itself to objects of desire, and it is not to be expected that it will be possible to wrench it away from them at once. A bamboo that has long borne a weight will not be straightened merely by its removal; strenuous effort will be required to neutralize the acquired bend. So it is with the mind. . . .
>
> *The Yoga of the Bhagavat Gita*, p. 55

Here the use of the will comes in. The work we wish to do now means a steady brooding on the subject; all its aspects must be included, its meanings and its implications, otherwise we shall achieve little more than our usual thinking. We must not permit any jumping to conclusions or one-sided examination. Neither should we allow our thinking to be coloured by emotions of any kind. The whole process must be kept under control, and it would serve good purpose to recall our old symbol of the controller and director—the charioteer.

The second precept is *persistence*. We are quickly apt to think we have uncovered all there is to the subject being considered, but must persist through this phase. It is a mental reaction. If need be, we can restimulate attention by reading something on the subject, by looking it up in a dictionary or by listing questions on it to which we should like an answer. The time for this reflective work should always be pre-determined and not made longer than we can expect to keep our minds on it. Five to ten minutes is ample to focus on one theme to begin with, and it is better to keep the time short and within our capacity, than to become discouraged by having asked too much of our minds.

Any subject chosen should be continued with each day for at least a week. Even a month may not be found too long. This compels us to reach into its depths. After all, this is why we meditate, to go below the surface, probe beyond the apparent, find the elements we otherwise would never know were there. Exponents of meditation in the East are said to devote even years sometimes to the contemplation of one subject. There are many accounts of faithful disciples obeying such injunctions which put our flitting efforts quite to shame!

No matter how simple may be the subject, if we persist with it there are always new significances to be found and deeper fields of comprehension to be arrived at. New realizations are the treasure trove of meditation, and in their pursuit we also add to the aptitude of our minds. Just as an athlete builds up his physical body through training, so the mind is flexed in reflective meditation and becomes more responsive, discerning and alert. Meditation is a dual enterprise; it repays through its achievement and its achieving. That these returns take place silently may at first make them less obvious. But we shall nevertheless find they are very real.

All kinds of subjects can be chosen for reflective meditation. As well as words and qualities, phrases may be used
which embody a thought of value or a concept which we
want to discover more about. Here are some examples that
could well be used:

'Be joyful, for joy lets in the light.'
'Harmlessness is not negativity, but perfect poise.'
'Pain is the swiftest horse that bears us to perfection.'
'The will-to-good is the magnetic seed of the future.'
'A point of tension is, symbolically, a storehouse of
  power.'
'Every moment the world and we are *renewed*.
  Life, like a stream of water is renewed and renewed,
  Though it wear the appearance of continuity in form.'

Such phrases are called 'seed thoughts' for the obvious
reason that they are capable of infinite development and, if
we choose constructive themes like those given here, they
will grow in our consciousness and flower out as we reflect
on them, thus imbuing us with their quality. We shall also
find out a great deal about them, for reflection is a potent
means of revelation.

Symbols are also valuable for reflective meditation and an
example of how they can be used in this way follows. As
will be seen in the exercise, visualization plays a large part if
a symbol is used because its whole purpose is the portrayal of
meaning and significance in form. It will also be seen how
this can then be related to a deeper purpose and the meditation become elevated to individual (or group, or world)
spiritual unfoldment.

Outline for a reflective meditation on a lotus

I PREPARATION
   Relax and make a rapid alignment, as gone into in
   Chapter VI.

II VISUALIZATION
   Imagine a closed lotus bud. Visualize the shape of
   the bud resting on its broad green leaves on the
   water. Picture the smooth texture of its petals and
   their yellow or white closely folded form. Next,
   visualize the bud opening very slowly, revealing
   petal after petal, as each unfolds. As the flower
   opens wider, see its full beauty emerging and its
   golden centre radiating in the sun.

III RECOGNITION
   Hold this picture of the open lotus for a few
   minutes with a sense of joy and admiration.
   Recognize it as a symbol of inner growth,
   unfoldment and expansion. Consider the
   significance of its roots being in the mud, its stem
   in the water and its flower in the air and the sun.

IV REFLECTION
   Reflect on the correspondence between the Self
   and the lotus with its hidden potentialities for
   growth, harmonious development and radiation.
   See how the life within the lotus resembles the
   emanation of the Soul or Self, unfolding through
   the form and expressing its essence, quality and
   aims.

V REALIZATION
   Realize that the Soul can unfold through you, just
   as the petals of the lotus open out. Identify

yourself with this symbol of the Soul for a minute and see the petals as qualities to be expressed in daily life.

VI AFFIRMATION

Close the meditation by anchoring or 'earthing' the inner work you have done with the words: 'So let it be. And may I be helped to fulfil my part.'

This is but one example of a reflective meditation and usually visualization would not play so large a part. But an outline of this nature makes a good 'first' meditation, because visualization undoubtedly aids the focussing of the mind. A rose may be substituted for the lotus if preferred, and other symbols can be used in much the same way.

Djwhal Khul, who has taught and written extensively on meditation, speaks of it having two general aims:

a. The formulation of thoughts, the bringing into form on the concrete levels of the mental plane of abstract ideas and intuition. This, he writes, might be termed 'meditation with seed.'
b. The aligning of the personal vehicle and creation of a vacuum, or unimpeded channel, between the physical brain and the higher Self or Soul, which results in a divine outpouring. This he terms 'meditation without seed'.

At a certain point the two blend, but to begin with, they should be understood and practised separately, and this may clarify what sometimes appears ambiguous in the different instructions about meditation that we find. Into the first category come the different kinds of *reflection* we have just been examining—meditation on a seed thought or a symbol. The second category we come to now with *receptive meditation.*

This is a more difficult type and takes us to the precincts of the higher, more advanced, abstract meditation carried out by those of long experience. But we can at least begin with its preliminaries and should find it helpful at times when we need higher guidance and are seeking insight on a problem.

Certain dangers are attached to this type of meditation; the human mind is already exposed to countless thought currents, impressions and impacts of all kinds, and care must be taken that negativity to them is not increased. But it will be obvious that unless we achieve *right* receptivity, we shall get little further than mental activity in meditation; also it is patent that the mind must be stilled from even the highest activity for Self realization to be reached, and for any higher communion to be two-way and effective.

Recognition of the 'sea' of impacts which buffets us continually is, in a way, a valuable by-product of receptive meditation. It helps us to realize the endless stream of impressions to which we are exposed subtly and unconsciously as well as consciously. And knowing this should put us on our guard and help us to develop some protection from the individual, group or family and mass influences which are constantly impinging.

These influences are on emotional as well as mental levels and may reach us through the senses, through psychic impressions and telepathically on mental levels, as well as through the more tangible means of which we are already aware, like the press, radio and television. We all know, too, the mass excitement that can sweep through a crowd and the waves of fear that cause mass panic, or of anger that can lead to uncontrolled destruction; also the power that words and ideas can have when 'put over' by a Hitler. Advertising is another 'bombardment' to which we are exposed, and its subtle power to influence was recognized abruptly a few years ago through the discovery of the effect of subliminal advertising.

But there are subtler currents from many different sources making their impact on both the thought substance in which we think and the astral substance in which we feel, sense and pick up psychic impressions—whether consciously or not. This is where we may frequently make mistakes, not knowing if our thinking is our own or is influenced by some extraneous source, not being able to discern whether an impression is of a high and true origin or simply a psychic distortion we have caught on the astral planes.

There are no quick answers to this situation, which presents increasing problems as the race as a whole is gaining greater sensitivity and awareness, and consequent receptivity to these impacts. But these factors should be recognized, for we cannot live in psychic isolation. To do this, even if we were able to, would mean being completely self-centred, and the paranoic is the extreme example of those who have tried to defend themselves in this isolationist way.

The solution lies in developing our own strong centre of awareness, *from which* we look out on the subjective as well as objective worlds around and attempt to control, to refuse or permit, the subtler impacts much as we would visitors to our home. This may well be a long process, but it is part of the building done through meditation and as we practise this receptive type, we shall become more familiar with these problems and able to handle them with more expertize.

The first point to recognize is the hair line path between an over-positive attitude and one that is too negative, between action and stillness, between mental creativity and passive absorption. The point of right tension has an element of both negative and positive and this can perhaps best be made clear by comparing receptive meditation to trying to hear a distant sound. For this, we physically keep still, silent, with breath held, yet we are far from negative, for every nerve is strained to catch the faintest sound.

So it is on the subtler planes. We do not want to be tense

physically, of course, holding our breath, but a certain tension must be achieved—which is different from tenseness. The receptive, or negative, listening attitude needs to be blended with positive attention to bring about the right point of tension, which then makes extension possible. It is a high point of achievement; we may grope for it for long before attaining it, and even then may only be able to hold it momentarily. 'One cannot remain forever on tiptoe', as Lao Tzu put it, and even such great practitioners of meditation as St Gregory and St Augustine were saddened that they could not maintain withdrawal from sensations and thoughts for as long as they wished to.

To quote Sri Krishna Prem again, who may be considered to be among the best authorities:

Essentially the method consists of gaining such control over the mind-processes that they can be stilled at will, thus enabling the consciousness to perceive the Truth like a calm lake reflecting the eternal stars. . . . The state is not one of mental vacuity, as represented by some critics, and still less is it one which is produced by some 'occult' mechanism or other. The centre of consciousness withdraws its attention from the world of outer phenomena, whether of sense or of thought, passes through the central point, which is itself, and emerges in the spiritual world of the *buddhi*.*

The Yoga of the Bhagavat Gita, pp. 49, 52

Paul Brunton makes the same point when he writes:

Mere mental quiet is an excellent thing as a step on the upward way but it is not true transcendence. The mental blank which is so often the absorption state of ordinary yogis is not the same as the self-understood

* Realm of intuition.

awareness which is the absorption state of the philosophic yogi. . . . The diffuse, drifting negativity of the first is inferior to and different from the discriminating, intelligent alertness of the second. The one merely refrains from thinking. The other actively engages the thought-free consciousness in understanding its own nature.

The Wisdom of the Overself, p. 257

So also warn certain ancient rules for aspirants compiled in Tibet: 'The stillness of inactive thought-processes (in the individual mind) may be misunderstood to be the true goal, which is the stillness of the infinite Mind.'

These are, of course, comments on high states that we cannot yet expect to reach, but at the same time it is good to have our goal clearly in mind, and perhaps in all these explanations the phrase '*thought-free consciousness*' is one of the most revealing.

Yet the path is strewn with what may at first appear to be contradictions, and the beginner is told that, to start with, one of the most important precepts of receptive meditation is to keep the consciousness on the mental level. For this reason it must be preceded by the usual preparation and a deliberate focussing of attention on the planes of the mind. A good way of doing this is to spend a few minutes reflectively meditating before attempting to reach a state of receptivity. This will consolidate the needed mental polarization and positive attitude.

To hold a state of *positive* listening silence takes a sustained act of the will. Most will find they have to strive for every level of it they may eventually attain, and it is generally accepted that we cannot—until really experienced meditators—keep all extraneous thoughts at bay. The very setting up of a point of silence invites a flood of sensations or impressions or images to invade our privacy. The best technique is not to fight them, or this means we have truly been caught by their 'bait', but to let them play on the periphery of the consciousness without giving them attention, like ripples on the edge of a stream of water, or like half-noticed clouds in a summer sky, which drift along the horizon without interfering with our enjoyment of the sun.

The holding of this state is helped by repeating some word or phrase, or evoking some image, which suggests calm and quiet. The picture of a majestic mountain or a peaceful lake; words like 'serenity', 'tranquillity', 'silence'; repetition of a mantram like 'Be still and know that I am God'—all these help to maintain this state of mind. The attempt should not be made for too long at a time because, apart from increasing its difficulty, we may, if trying to be mentally still for too long, find drowsiness supervenes. This must not be permitted. It will not be conducive to catching higher impressions and may well lead us into a psychic, mediumistic state which can be dangerous. If we get sleepy, we should bring the meditation to a close at once.

Analogies are often helpful because they are pictorial, and one we might usefully consider here is the searchlight directed by the ground crew towards objects in the sky. In *reflective meditation*, the 'minds's eye' is directed more or less horizontally, sweeping across the fields of consciousness, correlating, formulating, interpreting and seeing more clearly the things in its domain. In *receptive meditation*, on the other hand, the mind's eye is directed upwards, like a searchlight scanning the depths of the sky, trying to discern what may be beyond the levels reached by normal sight. The modern radio-telescope offers another analogy which illustrates our position well; its response apparatus is a perfect example of what the meditator's ought to be.

Finally, what can we expect to receive through this 'listening'? We have several means of reception, and spiritual impressions may reach us through seeing, hearing, sense of contact and urge to action, as well as in other ways.

The seeing of light is a frequent phenomenon, although the high spiritual illumination spoken of in Chapter III should not be confused with the light that is likely to occur in meditation. We may have various experiences of light; we may see it in the head, or before the eyes, or as a suffusion; or we may be aware of it in the sense of enlightenment on an issue, or the lifting of the mind into a new 'illumined' area, where deeper insight or realization may be gained.

Intuition is comprehension on these higher levels. It is said to be 'the light that shines between the eyes, the voice that speaks in the silence of the heart', and we might add 'in the heart of silence'. It is a high state of enlightened responsiveness. The word is loosely used when we get a 'hunch' or psychic impression, but true intuition is of an altogether higher domain.

An attempt should always be made to assess the origin and level of any impressions we receive. Colours and images, for instance, frequently appear, but they are the product of the imagination, they are not mental in origin, and therefore should be given no attention when they occur.

Hearing is also a frequent means of reception, an 'inner' hearing, in which, again, we must try to discriminate between what may be psychic voices and messages which genuinely come from the Soul. The latter may be 'silently heard', or ring like a clear voice speaking, but they are invariably short, clear, incisive, and generally deal with our spiritual life. Another way of distinguishing them is that they seem to 'ring a bell'—we recognize them as something true. Music also may be heard. Many of the great composers have more or less simply written down the music which they 'heard'. Mozart, for example, is said to have remarked that writing music caused him no difficulty, it simply seemed to come pouring forth and he only had to write it down.

The *presence* of the Soul—another form of response—is sometimes a very real experience. It leaves us with a feeling of new energy, of renewal, strength, courage, certainty, which is unmistakable, and the experience is coloured with a joy that no personal pleasures bring. Soul contact may take place in varying degrees, and although it is, of course, an objective in all meditation, it may not often be realized to the extent just mentioned until we have carved out a channel of communication with our higher Being to at least a certain extent.

Brother Lawrence is a famous example of how this may be achieved so that, in the end, the 'presence' is known in the midst of even the most mundane aspects of our lives. But we should remember that he gave his life over to achieving this, and to begin with we must be content with a fleeting gesture now and then as promise from the Soul of what the future holds.

There are reasons for this, apart from our inadequacy or unpreparedness. It is obvious that we may not always provide the right vibration for contact to be possible; also, too much of the Soul—as of any good thing—might have unexpected and over-stimulating effects. But we may suppose also that the Soul is frequently occupied with its own higher affairs. Meister Eckhart wrote:

> Philosophers say the Soul is double-faced, her upper face gazes at God all the time and her lower face looks somewhat down, informing the senses; and the upper face, which is the summit of the Soul, is in eternity and has nothing to do with time; it knows nothing of time or of the body.

The Master Djwhal Khul also has said that the Soul has little awareness of the personality nature, its disposition and ideas. It is conscious of the limitations within the personality and the barriers opposed to the inflow of Soul energy, but the details of the lower nature, he makes clear, are not the concern of the Soul. It is occupied with its own work on more spiritual levels, recognizing, registering and responding to the down pouring energies and ideas that will meet world need and aid mankind.

The urge to action is yet another manifestation which may result from meditation. It is also a natural effect of any of the foregoing forms of 'revelation', for if we genuinely receive an impression from a higher source, energy is bound to be transmitted with it, which we shall feel the urge to express. While it is a necessary completion of the meditative process to anchor or 'earth' this energy and utilize it in some specific way, we can easily fall into a trap here. Some lower wish or even unconscious element in the middle or lower unconscious (see the diagram in Chapter III, p. 39) may be stimulated by the energy received and rise up, using the disguise of 'holiness' to assert itself. The inner worlds are all too apt to glamour us, and we fall into the trap of giving our personal motives some high, 'divine' origin. Dramatic injunctions that we have a high calling should always be regarded with suspicion. The subconscious can play all kinds of tricks!

The main criterion for assessing the level of impressions is their impersonality. Messages that 'boost' the personality, that flatter and hold high promise we may always suspect as distortions. It is said that on the higher reaches of the Path the Master is rarely concerned with the disciple's personal life; his instructions are confined to the work to be carried out, the personality being the disciple's own responsibility. On the humble level of the beginner, we can therefore be very sure that we shall not receive divine injunctions from the Masters. Our own Soul is the medium to whom we must look for light. The Soul is sometimes called the 'first Master', and it is to this Fragment of Divinity that we should direct the inner ear.

Finally, over-stimulation should be watched for and guarded against with wisdom. The effect of meditation is almost always stimulating, and even the purest and most spiritual energy can have a devastating effect if it streams into the personality vehicles with too much force. Emotionally, nervously, physically and mentally it can either exhaust or feverishly stimulate. It has been likened to a sudden flow of increased current along the wires of an electrical installation which will cause any weak parts to fuse and burn out. At any signs of over-stimulation, therefore, meditation should be stopped immediately, or at least curtailed for a time.

The results of meditation do not always occur at once. They may be delayed for days or even months. Just as when we have been unable to recall something, and it drops at an apparently unconnected moment suddenly into the mind, so it is sometimes with the effects of meditation. We may suddenly get an idea, or thought, or even a direct injunction which answers or is a guide to a long held problem. The workings of the unconscious are still a mystery, and it seems that things get delayed sometimes on its higher levels before they reach the conscious level, where we wait.

It should also be remembered that we are part of a 'collective unconscious' of which little is yet understood. This may often account for 'answers' which reach us through other people, and also for results of inner searching which arrive in what seems a miraculous way.

After mention of all these possibilities, anyone who has had no 'manifestations' at all after receptively meditating for some time may well be rather cast down, feeling he is not achieving all he should. But discouragement need not be allowed to creep in; it really is not warranted. The silence may well indicate that the level of meditation is above all astral reactions and consequent 'demonstrations', and a little time is likely to be needed before there is sufficient mental attunement for pure mind reception. Of one thing the meditator can be assured; he is laying sounder foundations by steady, silent effort than is the recipient of exotic messages.

The real results of meditation lie far deeper—in its gradual building in, its raising of vibration, its cultivation of potential. These things are not to be measured by the more dramatic but temporary 'manifestations', which may encourage or—shame on us—flatter! But never must they be allowed to become our main concern. The fruits of meditation come slowly, but they come with an inevitable tide, and take us forward to a new world in their own sure and lawful way. We could well take to heart Arthur Clough's well-known lines:

> For while the tired waves, vainly breaking,
>   Seem here no painful inch to gain,
> Far back, through creeks and inlets making,
>   Comes silent, flooding in, the main.
>
> And not by eastern windows only,
>   When daylight comes, comes in the light,
> In front, the sun climbs slow, how slowly,
>   But westward, look, the land is bright.

To quote from *The Yoga of the Bhagavat Gita* again, if only the effort of the meditator is steady, his ultimate triumph is secure, and at last

> like a tree long bound by winter frosts, bursting suddenly into glorious bloom, the arduous struggles of many lives bear fruit and he will burst into the Light and attain contact with the Eternal, no longer sensed as a vague background, no longer even glimpsed fitfully through the inner door, but felt in actual contact, contact that will drench the soul in bliss.

The following example of a Receptive Meditation may be used as an outline into which we fit whatever receptive work we wish to do. It may be without 'seed' altogether, in which we simply seek the presence of the Soul. Or we may have a project or idea or problem upon which we hope to get inspiration or higher help. Alternatively, we may work with some form of world need like peace, right relationship, compassion, taking it into receptive meditation in order that higher ideas on it may perhaps come in. Because this, let us ever remember, is one of our functions as meditators amongst mankind, to provide 'receptive points' for spiritual or higher ideas to descend into the thought substance that we share with our fellow men. This, we shall go into further in Chapter IX, when we come to the service that meditation can fulfil. But it is good—perhaps encouraging too—to realize that meditation is less of an individual activity than we may have thought it to be.

The pool of reflection is not a private place, despite its intimate, deep silence. On these levels we are beyond our individuality and participating in substances and energies which pervade mankind. These areas of thought are no longer the little province of our personal thinking; they are the ethers where, it might be said, the 'thought of God' awaits humanity's acceptance. In the East they sometimes call this the region of 'the rain cloud of knowable things'. They speak, too, of the 'rainbow bridge'—a bridge built in consciousness—which must be built before we reach these high places.

Such concepts are both pictorial and symbolic—telling deeply of truths we cannot yet define. They help us to still our little selves before the immensity of the world we see from the shores of the pool of reflection, and they help us to forget ourselves before its vast proportions, so that we *know* —be it only for a moment or two—that we are citizens of the Infinite.

Outline for receptive meditation

I PREPARATION

Relax and make a rapid alignment and dedication as before.

II VISUALIZATION

Visualize a tranquil lake, set in a quiet place with trees upon its shore and high mountains in the background. Picture the reflective quality of the water. Realize that its capacity to catch on its surface the trees, mountains, clouds, symbolizes the capacity of the tranquil mind to catch the impressions available from 'above'.

III RECEPTION

Try to assume this receptive state, keeping control over the mind processes and holding the consciousness open to perceive or receive what it can of truth. Hold at the centre of focus the theme or subject on which you seek enlightenment. If necessary, repeat any words that help in doing this. Keep positive yet passive, alert, but mentally silent, listening, responsive to what may descend.

IV ANCHORING (or 'earthing')

Bring down into form, carefully and precisely, anything that has occurred to you. Meditate on it *reflectively* for a minute or two so that it becomes anchored in your consciousness and is clearly enough in mind to be made full use of. Write it down concisely, as this will 'earth' it further and ensure that it is not forgotten afterwards.

V AFFIRMATION

Send out a thought of gratitude for the help received even if this has been nothing more definite than a few minutes of quiet in the precincts of the Soul. Say, aloud if possible, to dedicate the result of the meditation and pledge yourself to its right use and expression:

'So let it be, and may I be helped to fulfil my part.'

Without the Potter turns his wheel
his work has no symmetry.
Unknown

VIII · THE WHEEL

The words of Christ reported by St Luke—'Ask, and it shall be given you; seek, and you shall find; knock, and it shall be opened'—framed a fundamental law which runs through the life of our planet—the law of demand and supply. They registered, if all too simply for our present intellectual outlook with its little faith, the basic premise that need, making itself known, evokes response from the universal 'storehouse', that a vacuum is inevitably filled when conditions are right and that effort sets in motion forces which bring about a corresponding return.

Because of the complexity of human life, we rarely see the results of prayer working out so simply. But the underlying principle of use, demand, supply remains constant; it is a law of spiritual as well as material economics, and the obstructing factors lie in ourselves. The riches of the kingdom of God are available, but we must link ourselves with the 'supply', must present our need rightly. This presentation acts like a cog-wheel in machinery and we become linked, like wheel does with wheel, with power upon power, part of an Olympian system.

The wheel reminds us constantly of energy set in motion, whether it is the wheels that speed movement, the interdependent wheels of machinery or the pulley wheels promoting give and take, demand and supply. It is therefore a helpful symbol of mankind's prayer, for, turning full cycle, it must transmit the energy with which it is synchronized. But the main lesson in the symbology is that, just as the connecting wheel of the water-mill has to be set in motion to use the power of the river sweeping by, so must we set the wheels of prayer turning for spiritual forces to come to our aid. They cannot flow in unless conditions make it possible. The initial act of alignment and appeal—no matter what we call it—must be made by *our* hearts and minds.

The framing of demand, be it physical, emotional or mental, or all three, creates an invocative current; it acts with pulling power, magnetically attracting that to which it is keyed. A channel is created by the focus, a magnetism is exerted by the need; and according to the level on which the appeal is made, so will be the quality of the response. Like attracts like, presenting a similar vibration which offers thus a channel for that which is sought. We may turn our prayer wheel dumbly, like the oxen hauling on the stone that grinds the corn, or we may attempt to link it with the heavenly motions and become part of the divine energy flow. But it rests with *us*, no matter what the form of appeal, to set the wheel in motion that will link us with the greater powers.

Prayer is the cry of the heart that recognizes forces greater than its own, and men have prayed since before the dawn of history. We do not know when the human being first thought of himself as an individual with forces surrounding him with which he must learn to work. Perhaps he never realized it precisely. But slowly, we may imagine, his innate awareness told him that powers were available beyond his own resources. So appeal for help began. First our ancestors probably asked the Source of the rains to slake their thirst, of power to give them strength in battle, of life to protect them from misfortune. From this would grow the kind of bargaining that pleased their fellow men and sacrifice was offered to gain more favour that more help might come. So, prompted by need, but also born of a certain rude observance of the law of give and take, developed the elaborate rituals of petition and propitiation such as are still to be found among primitive tribes.

Need has changed down the ages, but it has not diminished and at every stage spiritual leaders have tried to teach mankind how to pray. But it has been hard for us to follow its laws implicitly, encompassed as we are by our 'selfness', and our defaulting, like the little leaks in a dam, deprives us increasingly of this potential power. So we slip further out from what G. Granger Fleming called most cogently 'in line with the great sequences'.

It is not our purpose to study prayer here, but we need to understand its function in relation to meditation. Generally speaking, it is the appeal of the heart in petition or intercession or worship, whereas meditation is a function of the mind. But the prayerful attitude is an essential part of the practice of meditation, which needs to be motivated by the heart as well as head and be lifted on the wings of a certain dedication.

Prayer has varied to meet the changing needs and varying psychology of different times and peoples, but few would deny the part it has played in the growth of our civilization. Perhaps no single factor has touched so many lives or fulfilled so great a rôle in our history, and we shall never know what it has wrought or the measure of the service of the contemplatives through the centuries.

But basically, prayer has been a method of supplication, of asking God to come to our aid, and this has sent it out of fashion amongst the younger generations. The idea of benign 'handouts' from an ever-listening Father figure makes no sense to the modern mind. The urge to freedom is also too strong to accept such dependence or recognition of authority. But perhaps the personalization of God is the greatest cause of this repudiation, and this is understandable. It offends the sense of law and logic and the scientific approach so loved today.

Yet some form of prayer will always be needed. As long as we are on the evolutionary path, that is, on the way towards the divinity that will one day be ours, we shall need to invoke in some way that which is greater than ourselves. We shall always resort in our inmost selves to some kind of higher communion whenever faced with crisis, fear, uncertainty, despair, and in our high moments of joy and gratitude. Such times shake the walls of our isolation and show its pitiful proportions; they literally 'bring us to our knees' and to recognition again and again that we must learn to co-operate with the powers that surround us. So we are bound to develop new forms for our appeal to them—new forms that will satisfy our querulous minds as well as frame the need that our hearts feel.

This is, today, being done to a considerable extent as the pinch of spiritual poverty is gradually being felt throughout our culture and 'civilizing' processes. All kinds of meditation and ways of achieving contact with the subtler world are being explored and a new 'science of invocation' is emerging. But before going on to that, we must take note of another function that prayer has fulfilled down the ages, for this, too, must be replaced if prayer is being discarded.

Prayer is more than simply an act of asking. It is a lifting up as well as a calling down. Among its many components are dedication, thanksgiving and recognition of a higher or greater power. These attitudes are all redeeming, transmuting, lifting in influence; prayer consecrates if properly carried out. It has a redemptive effect on both that which is prayed for and the one who prays.

This is deeply hidden in what Teilhard de Chardin called 'mystical science . . . the science of Christ running through all things', and its truth is only revealed through penetration into this. Mostly we are apt to use our various forms of approach to the inner world superficially, from habit or when in urgent need, and their wider, deeper function and significance pass us by. In his thoughts on the *Mass on the World*, Teilhard de Chardin gives an immense yet immediately practical concept of the redeeming work that prayer can carry out:

It seems to me that in a sense the true substance to be consecrated each day is the world's development during that day—the bread symbolizing appropriately what creation succeeds in producing, the wine (blood) what creation causes to be lost in exhaustion and suffering in the course of its effort.

In *From Intellect to Intuition* Alice A. Bailey writes of the difference between prayer and meditation.

. . . It is asking, demanding and expecting which are the main characteristics of prayer, with desire dominant and the heart involved. It is the emotional nature and the feeling part of man which seeks after that which is needed, and the range of needs is wide and real. It is the heart approach. . . .
Meditation carries the work forward into the mental realm; desire gives place to the practical work of preparation for divine knowledge.   *p. 67*

In other words, to heart and feeling we add intellect, mental perception, and a new creativity is born. But we have yet another attribute that we can use—will—as we saw in Chapter V, and this brings us to *invocation*. This, in the modern usage of the word, is a method of spiritual appeal which, to quote Assagioli,

> includes and combines the use of all our inner functions. It is a simultaneous activity of the mind (meditation), of feeling (prayer), of the imagination (visualization), and of the will (affirmation). It is obvious that this comprehensive and synthesized action of our whole being, when rightly carried out, gives to invocation a potency incomparably greater and richer than the separate use of any single inner activity.

It is obvious, too, that this is not nearly as easy a method of aligning ourselves with and appealing to the inner forces as is prayer. It means using all the four faculties mentioned as an integrated whole. This is a new technique for most, but working with the different types of meditation touched on in the previous chapters will prepare the ground. Prayer, meditation, visualization and affirmation, although different and distinct, are inter-related, and each stimulates and facilitates the use of the others. When we have learnt to use each aspect of ourselves—heart, mind, imagination and will—separately, it is therefore easier to combine them and we soon become able to blend them and use them in a synthesized act of invocation.

This is patently a new age way of working and it has been said by the Tibetan writer quoted earlier, the Master Djwhal Khul, that

> Invocation is the highest type of prayer there is and the new form of divine appeal which a knowledge of meditation has now made possible.

He has also suggested that the new World Religion will be based on the science of invocation and evocation, which will provide a new dynamic medium for relating the inner and outer worlds.

There is food for thought in this concept, particularly because it is something which touches us all. We are the machinery of this communication, we form the cogs of all its wheels. It has to take place through us, the human kingdom. We are the intermediaries between light and darkness, God and animal, spirit and dense, unregenerate matter. To become better communicators, more proficient in relaying the powers of the spirit is therefore a major challenge to us all. It is also a responsibility we should recognize. The salvation of the world, the lifting of suffering, the establishing of peace, the changing and transmuting and enlightening of mankind rest with us greatly. They rest with us not simply in a general way and in the practical field, but in the quiet depths of our own hearts and the recreative power of our thinking.

In the vast mechanism of the human race it is easy to think that we do not matter, that our puny effort would hardly be missed, that our invocation or prayer cannot make any difference to the world. But we should be wrong to belittle our efforts. Each time we set the wheel of our inner communion turning, we are linking ourselves with infinite powers, with salvaging forces which we thus induct into the human aura, where they will do their own work.

As already said, invocation utilizes and combines the prayerful attitude of the heart, the meditative action of the mind and the focussed will or intention. The kind of will referred to here is of course the high, dedicated will which reflects the purpose of the Soul and is impelled by pure, unselfish motive, seeking only the good of the whole. A convinced mind, dedicated desire and planned activity are also essential parts of successful invocation. So is a certain sense of identification, for this is implicit in this type of appeal which infers not mere reception, but co-operation with the forces for which it is being made. To invoke we not only ask, we call forth, summon, see emerging, feel we can rightly demand and affirm. For example:

'Let the Forces of Light bring illumination to mankind!'
'May Peace prevail on earth!'

This is more than supplication; to the magnetic appeal of prayer is added all our other powers as well; we assert a rightful demand and the whole of our strength is involved. The presentation of need, the power of expectation, the acknowledgement of potential and the inner conviction that good will prevail are all part of the dynamic focus which makes invocation the most powerful means we can employ —if we use it rightly—to draw upon those high forces that can regenerate the world.

We may well expect that, just as prayer has been at the heart of religion in the past, so invocation will be at the core of the science of approach to spiritual powers in the future and will form the main foundation of the new World Religion we may look for in the Aquarian age.

A form of invocation which is now in use all over the world and is known as 'The Great Invocation' is given opposite because, not only is it a potent formula which we can use as a form of service, but it illustrates precisely the type of appeal which is properly called 'invocation'. It calls for three things needed by mankind; their source and where they are needed are both named; the word 'let' repeats both appeal and affirmation, and the whole is concise and mantric in vibration. These words can be said from the heart as a prayer, with the mind as a mental concept and with will that the forces invoked may prevail. Visualization can also add its contribution. These four methods, used together, constitute the essence of the 'science of invocation' and we can well employ the following formula as a contemporary means of saying our daily 'Mass for the World'.

The Great Invocation

From the point of Light within the Mind of God
  Let light stream forth into the minds of men.
    Let Light descend on Earth.

From the point of Love within the Heart of God
  Let love stream forth into the hearts of men.
    May Christ return to Earth.

From the centre where the Will of God is known
  Let purpose guide the little wills of men—
    The purpose which the Master knows and serves.

From the centre which we call the race of men
  Let the Plan of Love and Light work out
    And may it seal the door where evil dwells.
Let Light and Love and Power restore the Plan on Earth.

In all invocation the use of mantra plays an important part. It is a way by which we not only align ourselves with the spiritual forces addressed, but build a channel through which they may be expressed. A mantram is a collection of verses, phrases, words or sounds and might generally be called a prayer, but it usually has the added quality of rhythm and brings a certain vibratory power into play.

A mantram, it is said, when rightly sounded, creates a vacuum in matter which forms a channel of communication between the one who sounds it and the object of its appeal. This is the reason for the close guarding of the esoteric rites in ancient times. Power was released through the formulae used and to keep much of the ceremonies secret was a necessary safeguard. The inner rites were never divulged publicly, but handed down as a sacred trust only to those in whose charge they would be safely kept. This understanding must also have been the origin of the belief in spells, charms and so-called magical occurrences, which formed the themes of so many folk tales in the past.

From accounts in the Old Testament and other ancient scriptures, it seems that the priests knew very much more of the uses of sound in olden days than we do now—for instance the falling of the walls of Jericho. The rituals, chanting, singing and voiced prayer of religious services today are a very faint echo of the mantric forms used long ago. The use of mantra is more understandingly practised in the East today, and is spreading into the occident with some of the eastern forms of meditation now being taught here. These frequently include the use of words or sounds to aid concentration and establish a certain vibration, but this can be dangerous if done without knowledge and should only be practised under guidance one can trust.

Regarding the use of mantra, Aldous Huxley writes in *The Perennial Philosophy*:

> Just as traditional rites seem to possess the power to evoke the real presence of existents projected into psychic objectivity by the faith and devotion of generations of worshippers, so too, long-hallowed words and phrases may become channels for conveying powers other and greater than those belonging to the individual who happens at the moment to be pronouncing them.   *p. 329*

This is another encouragement for us, in our seeming isolation. A formula like, for instance, 'The Great Invocation' just quoted, which is used by thousands daily all over the world, can be a medium of great potency and our joining in its use can add much more to the volume of its appeal than our tiny individual effort might suggest.

But mantra act upon ourselves as well as within the more subjective realms. It has been said, for example, that the 'Great Invocation' with its appeal for illumination and love cannot be used without causing powerful changes in our attitudes, life intention, character and goals. 'As a man thinketh in his heart, so is he' is a basic law in nature; the constant turning of the mind to the need for light and love cannot help but have effect on us.

Modern psychology bears out the conditioning effect on the subconscious that this type of spiritual exercise must have, for considerable imprint on the unconscious as well as consciousness will be made if mantra or words of spiritual significance are repeatedly used. This has long been recognized by the great teachers and repetition of the divine name has been a widely practised exercise since earliest times. On a lower turn of the spiral, Coué utilized the same principle in his famous phrase 'Every day and in every way, I am getting better and better.'

Using a mantram will aid concentration, but too intensive or continued use of a word or phrase should be guarded against. It can lead to a kind of self-hypnosis and stupefaction. As with all forms of spiritual exercise, a right balance should be maintained. The Meister Eckhart gives yet another warning:

'He who seeks God under settled form lays hold of the form, while missing the God concealed in it.'

The use of mantra can, however, be a potent method of appeal and it may well be that more creative work is done by the repetition of such forms than is generally realized. Through sound we factually effect the ethers, through word forms we house the potencies of thought. The telling of beads, a universal practice in the East as well as in Christianity, is not only an act of devotion. It sets afoot a cycle of energy, making contact with the subtler forces possible. More power than we know lies hidden in the repeated *Pater Noster*, and perhaps the Tibetan prayer wheels hold more virtue than is realized in the West.

'Om mani padme hum' chants the eastern devotee, saluting the 'Jewel in the Lotus', which is his spiritual Self. So he identifies himself with it, raises and transfigures the lower consciousness. Also he builds through the rhythmic sound a channel of appropriate vibration for the spiritual energy he is saluting to connect with him.

Countless mantric forms of a similar nature are directed to the invocation of specific qualities and aspects. The polytheistic Hindu approach—which so horrified the Christian conscience —is an expression of this attempt to assimilate the qualities attributed to the different gods. It is in one way sound psychology; it invokes these qualities from high sources and establishes them in the consciousness—and subconscious—through thought, devotion and the attempt to identify with them.

Mantra form an important part of all spiritual communion, both ascending and descending, to use the two-dimensional terms with which we are apt to restrict the concept of subjective expansion. They aid the concentration of our forces and, as well as being scientifically or lawfully invocative, they imprint their message in the unconscious, from where we may expect it to condition us in various ways. They are a vital part of invocation, the wheels, we might say, which set it in motion.

Next we come to creative meditation. This demands a chapter on its own, yet we still might remember the symbol of the potter's wheel, for in creative meditation we gather all our resources to contribute to and build the subject concerned, we create a thought 'form' of it; then we set the wheel of prayer and invocation turning in order that greater energies may help to shape and be inducted into the form.

Like a merry-go-round, we are always involved in a great circle. We vary its pitch, its speed, its form, but we are always within the circuit that runs from inner to outer and back to inner again. The wheel of life, the circuit of energy, encompasses us in its universal arms and, dwarfed as we may be by its greatness, yet all potential lies within our reach because of its envelopment.

How long will you tread the circling tracks of mind
Around your little self and petty things?
A seer, a strong creator is within,
This transient earthly being, if he wills,
Can fit his act to a transcendent scheme.

AUROBINDO

IX · THE SERVICE OF MEDITATION

All meditation is a service of one kind or another, even meditation that is purely 'personal', for 'no man is an island entire of itself; every man is part of the continent, a piece of the maine.' All our lifting of ourselves to a higher level of being and entry into a wider area of consciousness is, therefore, a lifting of the whole, a service to our fellow beings, no matter how small.

But meditation can be a specific as well as general or pervasive form of service, and invocation and creative meditation are, like intercessory prayer, definite ways of rendering this. Invocation, as we saw in the previous chapter, has much more about it than we might expect. Now what is creative meditation?

This is not a different kind from those we have studied before; rather, it is like a many-sided diamond—a form that reflects the utmost light because of the many facets which are combined in it—and its practice is an ultimate service of all the meditation we have learnt to carry out. They have all been creative to a certain extent, but a planned 'creative meditation' is particularly effective because it utilizes the constructive aspects of the other kinds.

It will of course be obvious that we shall offend against spiritual law if we use creative meditation for selfish or materialistic ends. As we gain the power to work on subjective and more influential planes, it becomes increasingly important that we provide pure instruments, that is, channels that are unalloyed with self. We could neither contact nor be a medium for true spiritual forces, in fact, were our motives not rightly orientated. We should remember, therefore, that creative meditation should always be for some impersonal objective and be motivated by the desire to serve and to bring about the good of the whole.

It has been said that everything that eventuates on earth has first been born in the realms of the mind. Upon our right thinking, therefore, and the creative uses that we put it to, depends both what we make of ourselves and the world around. Since thought is an energy which we direct according to the way we order our thinking, it can be destructive as well as constructive, can build or despoil, help or hinder, and it is a force which we should handle with as much care as we do that of our emotions. The effects of thought are not seen as clearly as those caused by our more tangible feelings, and so we have not yet generally developed the sense of responsibility for our thinking that we automatically have for our emotions.

But we are beginning to see—and it is high time in our mentally galloping age—that thought is a tangible potency which creates, influences and has effect. We are recognizing, for instance, that it stimulates and adds momentum because we see how it feeds an anxiety or fear; who has not found that by continual thinking around some worry it has assumed gigantic proportions? And that fear builds up out of practically nothing if we permit it to be fed by thought? Put these things out of mind and they attrify and disappear.

So it follows that to think creatively on that which is

needed will build it and strengthen it from within. Destructive thought, on the other hand, has an undermining effect and even harms. It can be as destructive an energy on the mental level as is hate emotionally, and all know how tangible a wave of hate can be. It is difficult to dissociate thought and feeling, so we are apt to send our feelings out on the wings of thought without realizing we are doing so. This gives them added potency. This may not matter if our feelings are constructive, but even then, it is better to have both them and the volatile forces of thought under our conscious control.

Thought rightly used can recreate both ourselves and our surroundings. 'Be ye transformed by the renewing of your mind,' wrote St Paul to the Romans, and most of us miss out on much of our potential because of the little recreating that we do within our minds. We permit them a great deal of free range in unprofitable fields, whereas controlled use of them could harness valuable constructive energy. 'Think love' and we build it into ourselves; think of joy and we become more joyous. Thought links us with these great qualities and they naturally flow in and become stronger in ourselves.

Thinking creates what are called thought 'forms'. Intangible as they may seem compared with forms on the physical level, they are, nevertheless, coagulations of thought and are contributed to by all thought on them. In this way, mass thoughtforms are built up and become widely influential, the mass consciousness becoming impregnated with their quality or vibration.

This can be seen in the emergence of certain principles, teachings and trends at different times; even a vogue for some simple thing builds up from people's thinking, and advertising is built on the power of the influence of such thoughtforms. The more attention that is paid to them, the more influential they become. Everyone has probably had the experience of recognizing a thought current stronger than his own, and of having to struggle to maintain his own thinking, like a swimmer facing a strong tide.

To put it very briefly, the objective of creative meditation is to build the thoughtforms that are needed, and contribute to the strength and influence of spiritual qualities in this way. We do not necessarily initiate the thoughtforms that we work with because, if we are dealing with subjects like peace, compassion, enlightenment, they are already in existence in higher spheres. Our meditation is aimed at strengthening and clarifying them in the mental areas that we inhabit; they can then be more influential and be tuned in to with more facility by mankind—for we must remember that we share thought substance with our fellow men much as we share the air we breathe. It may be ours temporarily, but we share it in a subtle way, and a universal pool of thought substance encompasses us all despite our individuation. The diagrams in Chapters III and VI help to picturize this factor.

The interplay between the part and the whole is one of the mysteries not yet understood, but science is probing on its fringes now, investigating various lines of influence and response and the subjective link between part and part. Experiments in telepathy are being conducted in a number of fields. It is interesting to note that as we grow from emotional to more mental polarization, it is science rather than religion that is investigating and revealing the reality of higher communication and vertical as well as horizontal expansion.

So must the methods through which we seek to make our spiritual progress, communion and appeal also be on more mental levels now, and creative meditation may be expected to take the place, to a large extent, of feeling-promoted prayer. To quote that authoritative writer on the creativity of meditation, Djwhal Khul—

Words of power, ancient mantrams (such as the Lord's Prayer) and the Great Invocation are only effective if used upon the mental plane and with the power of a controlled mind, focussed on their intent and meaning, behind the spoken effort. They then become potent. When said with the power of the soul as well as with the directed attention of the mind, they automatically become dynamically effective.

For creative meditation the same initial procedure as for other forms can be used to orientate and dedicate ourselves to the work in hand. Then, having raised the consciousness to as near a point of identification with the Soul as possible, we begin to work with the chosen subject.

Let us suppose it is *Compassion*. First, we meditate on this quality *reflectively* (see Chapter VII), in this way gathering in our thoughts on it. This might be compared with compiling data for some project; we gather all the information we can, try to get a clear picture, formulate our ideas on how it functions, what its potentialities. This is, strictly speaking, the horizontal work. The thought directed to the subject and the foraging into its constituents, meaning and purpose helps to build and clarify it not only in our own minds, but as a 'thoughtform' in mental substance.

The next step is to meditate *receptively* (see Chapter VII again). This means we stop deliberate mental activity and hold the thoughtform as steadily and as far as we can within the light of the Soul. New ideas on Compassion can now drop down into the stilled, receptive thoughtform we are holding. Like an upturned chalice, we keep our concept of Compassion open, silent, waiting, in order that new spiritual meaning may flow in, or some deeper awareness of its significance or purpose become ours.

It is a mistake to try to hold this stage too long as we may then fall back into reflective meditation. True receptivity may only be reached for a moment or two. Then, in a flash of high identification, a new insight may be gained, or some revelation that will aid us to expedite its manifestation in the world. This may come from the Soul or from its own existing potency, but whichever it is, we can grasp it gratefully; it is a gift from the 'raincloud of knowable things'.

Now we move on to meditating *creatively*, that is, we direct thought once again, aided by the impressions just received, to building a deeper or richer concept of Compassion. All the thought and feeling that we can give to it helps to strengthen it on the ethers, helps to enlarge its image, make it more influential and more likely to enter the minds and hearts of humanity.

We can, for instance, visualize it changing certain conditions or situations and see it as a transmuting and saving force; we can so feel the need for it that we send it desire, love, heart energy as well as mentally appreciating its potential. By all this we are 'feeding' or 'energizing' it on all levels, helping to make it a vital, influential factor, and we open a vibratory channel to it along which it can flow with strength.

After this, we invoke it, using again the fourfold tools of prayerful attitude, creative imagination, focussed mind and affirming will. We ask for it, visualize it where it is needed, think of it redeeming, lifting, regenerating, while we assert that this can be. Finally we radiate it, trying to send it out on rays of lighted thought to aid its expression wherever it is needed.

When all this is spelt out it seems a long and laborious process, but once we get the habit of it, each stage can be covered in a very few minutes. A flash of thought can sometimes be much more potent in effect than a long meditation. The outline which follows summarizes the various stages and the length of these can vary according to what we find best.

A new form of meditation is always difficult at first because its sequence has to be remembered, but once this is mastered, a creative meditation is no more difficult than any other form for it is simply a combination of the others.

All through the succession of the world's spiritual teaching, it has been reiterated that spiritual appeal, whether we call it prayer, meditation or invocation, enables us to contact and draw upon inner energies and bring them to our help on earth. This has been a matter of faith in the past, but we can also see it as a process of synchronizing and attracting which works according to law. We set the wheel of creative thought in motion rightly and it gears us into the greater energy flow.

This is obviously a valuable form of service, and the giving of a few minutes to it every day seems not only a very worth while use of time and energy, but something urgently needed in our precarious times. And it is certainly a challenge to us to bestir ourselves, when we realize that we can play a definite part in helping to bring in the forces that the world so needs.

Outline for creative meditation

PREPARATION

Relax, establish a quiet rhythm of breathing and a calm throughout the physical body, feelings and mind.

DEDICATION

Make an act of alignment and dedication to the higher Self or Soul and its purpose.

REFLECTION

Begin by saying the word *Compassion*★ (it is often helpful to repeat this at each stage of the meditation). Reflect on it for a few minutes. Define it in various ways and try to arrive at a clear idea of what Compassion is and what it can do. (When a clear concept is reached, move on to the next stage. This keeps the meditation positive and creative.)

RECEPTION

Now lift the thoughtform of Compassion into the 'light' of the higher or superconscious. Try to hold it there for a few minutes, keeping an open, listening, receptive attitude. Note down any new idea or impression that drops in to the consciousness.

(Remember that at this stage it is impressions from the *higher* levels that are sought, not the product of the lower thinking.)

CREATIVE MEDITATION

With the help of the thought and impressions gathered in the two previous stages, now build a positive concept of Compassion. See its quality working out in some particular way in the world; imagine and visualize it influencing attitudes, changing situations. Consider how you can practically help its growth and emergence. Try to contribute with feeling as well as thought to its expression in some tangible way.

★ *Or whatever may be the theme of the meditation.*

INVOCATION

Frame in your own words the concept you have been working with and, using the energy of the will, affirm —aloud if possible—

May Compassion motivate the minds and hearts and action of humanity.

So let it be.

The service we can give through meditation is illustrated in another way by a widely used form of Meditation for the United Nations. In this the focus is given to that assembly of the countries of the world upon whose efforts the establishment of peace and international co-operation so greatly depends. We give it our subjective support and try to hold it in light, invoking through it the peace so needed by mankind.

Several years ago, a small group started doing this with the suggestion 'We can be delegates through thought'. Since then, a great number have joined in this project, sending their thought from all over the world constructively and expectantly (expectation is a valuable aid to creative thought), invoking wisdom and enlightenment for all those working there.

In the Headquarters building of the United Nations in New York is a Meditation Room. This was designed by Dag Hammarskjold as a place of quiet where those of all religions or of none could go to commune with whatever inner Power they recognized. It is a room of silence, where all who work at the United Nations, or who visit it, may go to attune their thinking with Reality, no matter by what name it is called.

In this room is a central block of iron ore, which might be called an altar, and upon it streams a shaft of light from an unseen source overhead. This symbolizes the light that *can* come in to illumine the affairs of the world, and in this form of creative meditation we can visualize this shaft of light reaching into the minds of all who work in the Council Chamber and who are seeking to guide and aid the destiny of mankind.

We can visit this room on the wings of thought at any time of the day, and a few minutes spent there, in company with the great band all over the world who are doing the same thing, can help to provide an inestimable force for good. From our own physical and spiritual meditation 'centre' we can work along the following lines:

Meditation for the United Nations

Entering the Meditation Room in thought, stand for a moment in its silence.

Imagine it as a central point of the councils of the world.

Visualize the room, with its symbolic altar in the centre and the shaft of light streaming upon it steadily from above.

Picture this light irradiating the minds of all those working in the Assembly and all who are in places of responsibility.

Holding this thought, send them goodwill as well as light, asking for wisdom and compassion to illumine them in their work.

Next, visualize this light and goodwill radiating out to all countries, peoples, places of conflict, crisis, suffering and need. See it resolving the difficulties, lifting the suffering, and after a minute's meditation on this, say, aloud if possible, the following invocation or any other prayer that may be chosen.

> May the Forces of Light bring Illumination to mankind.
> May the Spirit of Peace be spread abroad.
> May the Law of Harmony prevail.

May men of good will everywhere meet in a spirit of
co-operation.
So let it be and help us to do our part.

Yet another form of service we can give through meditation is to support those in places of leadership throughout the
world. A heavy burden rests upon their shoulders, they are
faced with making decisions that will affect the whole of
mankind, and they are trying to guide their nations rightly
while, at the same time, being under the bombardment of
the thought, feeling, criticism of perhaps millions at times.
Theirs is an unenviable task and even though we may not
agree with them, we can send them a constructive wave of
thought and attempt to surround them with light.

A word of warning should be said here. We should never
try to influence those in places of power. We cannot know the
true depths of the situations they are dealing with and cannot
know the rightful issue of any particular problem. We can
invoke the light they need to make right decisions, we can send
them goodwill, but what they do we must leave to them.

The same applies to situations in the world. We cannot
know the right outcome of any crisis, we can only ask that
it may come about. The true solution may be very different
from what we think and events may be part of a long evolutionary pattern that we know nothing about. Our task as
meditators is to work with energies, not events, to invoke
enlightenment and wisdom for those concerned, to radiate
love, to maintain calm and always remain confident that
right will prevail.

Perhaps one of the greatest contributions we can make is to
stand steady 'behind the scenes', helping to keep the channel
open for the Forces of Light to come in. In times of crisis,
conflict, suffering, there is apt to be a great deal of emotional

turbulence and a meditative service that those with any contact with their Souls can give is to tranquillize the ethers through their meditation and radiate the serenity of the Soul.

William James, philosopher and psychologist, wrote:

> Worry means always and invariably inhibition of associations and loss of effective power. . . . The turbulent billows of the fretful surface leave the deep parts of the ocean undisturbed, and to him who has hold on vaster and more permanent realities the hourly vicissitudes of his personal destiny seem relatively insignificant.

On Vital Reserves

So, in world as well as personal crises, those who know the Soul will be able to stand serene, facing the issues and the suffering, yet also knowing the distant horizon and the ultimate power of Good. Jan Smuts was once asked, in the midst of a time of acute crisis, what could be done by people to help. 'Give us the atmosphere in which we can work!' was his reply. This is one of the great forms of service we can give through meditation, establishing calm and working confidently to invoke the forces needed by those concerned.

If we can do this, for even a few minutes in the day, the divinity in us is not being idle. We are using our forces to help to bring about the Purpose and Plan we may not know, but which we are part of and are required to implement with all the 'God' in us that we can command.

The New Age is being born rapidly today, with all the attendant difficulties and crises. Creative meditation to build the spiritual structure on which it must be based is urgently needed. If we all resolve that in *some* way we will give *some* time each day to this end, we shall be helping to set afoot a tremendous power for building these true foundations for the age ahead and helping to lift the suffering of mankind.

'I am Brahma.' Whoever knows this, 'I am Brahma,' knows all. Even the gods are unable to prevent his becoming Brahma.

The Upanishads

X · BENEDICTION

In a letter to a friend, Rabindranath Tagore wrote:

> It is I who bloom in the flowers, spread in the grass,
> Flow in the water, scintillate in the stars,
> Live in the lives of men of all ages.

This sense of union, of oneness with the living essence that floods through the whole manifested universe, is something many have felt in some degree at one time or another. But such moments are the rare flashes of escape from the limitation of our selfhood and, normally, because of all the pressures round us, this awareness never rises up from the silent spring where it lies hidden in the depths of our being.

So we remain almost unaware through a large part of life of this basic, glorious, all-offering and all-absorbing partnership which we have in the universe. Sometimes we pay lip service to it; sometimes it is near enough to the surface to break through to a certain degree and temporarily over-ride the divisiveness of personal life, and undoubtedly it whispers against the irksomeness of brick walls, daily routine and perpetual encompassment by petty things. But rarely is it the reality to us that is spoken of in the writings of poets, philosophers, mystics, saints and all who have reached its supreme moments.

Browning wrote:

> Earth's crammed with heaven
> And every common bush afire with God,
> But only he who sees takes off his shoes.

We might also say that only he who takes off his shoes sees, for until we come to address ourselves to wider domains, look up from our small preoccupations and acknowledge the ineffable greatness with which we are surrounded, we go along blindly, nose to ground, like any mole with no day sight or totally absorbed hunting dog. Just as the wheel of prayer has to be set in motion, so we have to give house-room to the things beyond what seem to be our containing walls, must draw back the curtains from the windows of the little self so that the daylight can come in.

> Man can never reach the blazing centre of the universe simply by living more and more for himself, nor even by spending his life in the service of some earthly cause, however great,

wrote Teilhard de Chardin. It must involve 'a reversal, a turning about, an *excentration*'.

We move towards this realization of oneness in many ways. Music, art, poetry, scientific discovery and revelation, nature and beauty in all its forms—these are all avenues that link us with the all-pervasive Being of which we are fragmentary reflections. They are all channels along which we may pursue fuller experience of it, hasten the slow tread of natural evolution, reach our destined consciousness more quickly, and many of the great exponents in these fields have shown a supreme sense of this unification.

Even the great teachers of religion have hardly told of it more vitally than the poets and we know that it was the deep, motivating urge behind the production of a great many of the masterpieces in all fields of art. Beethoven had the words 'I am all that is—that was—that will be' framed on his desk. It was Tennyson who wrote 'Closer am I than breathing, nearer than hands and feet.' And William Blake's lines are well-known:

> To see a World in a Grain of Sand
> And a Heaven in a Wild Flower,
> Hold Infinity in the palm of your hand,
> And Eternity in an hour.

The examples are legion, but of all the ways by which we cultivate our sense of oneness with universal Life, meditation is the most direct Path. It is the way by which we set our faces determinedly towards it, harness our various forces to achieve it and use the tried and ageless methods that can expedite it. So far as any such personally-to-be-discovered way is definable, we could say that meditation is the defined path towards the benediction of knowing our oneness with God.

The sense of unification is both the impulse and the goal of our meditative work. Whatever we possess of it urges us on to possess more; whatever we experience of it impels us to achieve greater participation. Almost like a divine intoxication, our potential divinity draws us on—the more of it we attain, the greater its attraction. The point of response in us answers more and more insistently as we step nearer to the Source of the Great Magnetism. Rabindranath Tagore has spoken of it as 'the eternal play of love in the relation between this being and the becoming' and he illustrates it pictorially:

In the music of the rushing stream sounds the joyful
assurance, 'I shall become the sea'. It is not a vain
assumption; it is true humility, for it is the truth. The
river has no other alternative.

Through many ages the great method of linking with our
Creator has, of course, been religion, but we do not always
need established forms for our most personal—or more
accurately, 'non-personal'—experiences. In fact it is frequently only after discarding acknowledged means and
forms that we reach through to essences and realities and
find that we 'belong in' something which no amount of
trying to enter has ever brought us to so clearly. It is a time-
less and placeless entry into new dimensions of realities and
all the sages—eastern and western, ancient and modern—
have attested to this aspect of it in their different ways. Christ
taught that we must lose ourselves to find ourselves; the
Hindu scriptures speak of experiencing the Eternal now, and
in another way the same concept is put forward by the
Rabbi Pinhas of Koretz:

People think that they pray before God. But it is not so.
For prayer itself is the essence of the Godhead.

Paul Brunton uses the word 'Grace' for what he calls 'the
essential prerequisite' for this attainment. In *The Secret Path*
he writes:

. . . something more than conforming to a prescribed
system is required. And that final but important
ingredient he himself is powerless to supply. . . . The
awakening to spiritual consciousness is something which
cannot be developed by a mechanical and measured
system alone. 'Art happens!' declared Ruskin, and so
does spirituality. The aspirant carries on certain
practices . . . and one day the true consciousness seems

to come to him, quietly, gently but surely. That day
cannot be predetermined. It may come early in his
efforts; it may come only after long years of
disappointing struggle, For it depends upon a
manifestation of Grace from the Overself, of a force
deeper than his personal will, which now begins to take
a hand in the celestial game. Once the Grace gets to
work upon a man, there is no escape.   *p. 158*

Forms are useful in that they provide a framework, or
perhaps a better analogy would be a passageway along
which we proceed until we reach, in consciousness, the open
space to which it leads. Here, on the momentum we have
gathered through our long efforts in the passageway, the
'momentum of stillness', we then perhaps achieve some
experience of what lies ahead of us.

Yet these concepts should not lead us to think that it is
only beyond ourselves that we must look to reach a sense of
God and unification.

Hold, whither doest thou run?
Heaven is within thee. If thou seekest God elsewhere,
   then thou wilt miss Him.

So wrote Angelus Silesius and spiritual teachings repeatedly remind us of this point. Heaven is within as well as
without; divinity is omnipotent and in the heart's core;
God is transcendent and immanent. In the past we have
tended to emphasize the transcendent aspect of divinity, the
all-pervading, all-powerful God; but it is the God *in* everything, our essential divinity, which should be recognized,
for this factuality of God, this essence in all life can open our
minds to what only the heart has known before.

Modern science is playing a great part in awakening us to
this recognition, and through its revelations of the nature of

substance and energy it is spelling out to our concrete minds the truth of the ancient scriptures, the truth, for instance, of these words in the *Upanishads*, which were written centuries before the Buddha, Christ and perhaps even Moses:

> Vast is that, Its form unthinkable.
> Yet it shines smaller than the smallest.
> Far and farther than farness is It,
> Yet it rests in the heart's heart.

The spiritual path is paved with paradoxes, apparent contradictions which yet hold in their depths secrets which stand as sentinels, guarding the approaches to wider fields. Only when we have discovered their hidden reconciliation do we reach a true point of balance. This point is, like the apex midway above the scales, only attained through long experience of trial and error; it offers a steady vantage point. Through long experiment, weighing, testing, trying, leaving, alternating and reassessing, we emerge, at last, serene.

So we pursue our way, scanning the horizon, extending our concepts, yet knowing we must also search within. We pray, aspire, strive to make the needed spiritual endeavour, yet are also taught that we must stand silent, stilled and effortless to enter pure Being. We also orientate ourselves to the Soul, yet recognize that we shall only reach Soul infusion when we put our fellow men before ourselves.

'Action in inaction' we must learn; self-knowledge has to be attained as well as self-forgetfulness; mindfulness must be achieved as well as mindlessness. The God within is to be discovered as well as God Universal. As the spiritual paradoxes unfold before us, they pave our way.

On every level these discoveries of God must be made. From experience of union emotionally—the mystical ecstasy so frequently told of in religious history—to mental penetration and perception and, eventually, identification attained in intuitional realms. On all these levels, through all these means we reach our various grades of 'knowing' and unification and proceed towards that experience which Edith Sitwell framed in the words:

> The unborn God in the human heart
> Knows for a moment all sublimities.

But no matter at what stage our experience of union may be, meditation remains the most direct path. It is this way which leads us most unerringly not only into the realms of higher experience, but to develop in ourselves the quiet rhythm that will establish these more rarefied atmospheres in our consciousness. Each time we meditate, we might say that a little more of the causeway that leads across from world to world is established. We build this causeway with the substance of our own experience, knowing, consciousness, and, although we are greatly helped and encouraged by those who have achieved it before us and those doing so around us, yet we must each fundamentally build it of and for ourselves—out of the substance of our own awareness. All that we grasp in our higher moments we place under our feet; in the words of an ancient catechism:

> I toil; I serve; I reap; I pray;
> I am the Cross; I am the Way;
> I tread upon the work I do;
> I mount upon my slain self. . . .

Group meditation should be mentioned here, as this analogy of building a causeway of ourselves yet also helped by those around us illustrates the interplay of group and individual. It is often easier to meditate in the company of others and group meditation has an extra value, a 'plus' factor beyond the sum total of each individual's contribution.

This is because, when meditating in a group, we each bring our own quota, yet are also able to stand on the groundwork which has been built by our fellows. The vibration they are establishing, the impulse of their forward going are aids to our progress also, and meditation with others, if it is united on a common theme, can be extremely helpful and a powerful medium for creative and invocative work.

This brings us, finally, to the service of Blessing. As with the creativity of meditation, so its benediction also has a two-way flow and blesses both the one to whom it is directed, or who is held in its aura, and the one who meditates. When we succeed in offering the right receptive medium and invocatory vibration, the beneficence of the Soul is ours; healing, strengthening, 'spiritualizing' forces pour in and through the channel we create. These can be radiated in the measure in which they are received, indeed, we radiate what we are and have in us whether we know it or not. Therefore, some part of our meditation must reach out to others and to our environment, must spread its quality and benediction.

But we can do more than that. We can deliberately radiate the spiritual forces with which we make contact, can channel them—act as 'transmitting stations'. We may hardly be able to send them out with a 'switch-on' efficiency, but we may have more pervasive power than we are aware of, and shall be able to bless, strengthen, heal, lift, according to the channelship that has been built.

This should be remembered as one of the great goals of meditation. Not only can we—and must we—turn to the Soul, our spiritual Mentor, for guidance, instruction, strength and all we need for our own benediction, but we can become agents for the storehouse of the Spirit, inter-mediaries able to bring some measure of the treasures of the kingdom of heaven to earth for mankind. We can, in fact, set up an 'agency' for whatever kind of treasure we choose;

love, wisdom, joy, compassion, light, goodwill—there is no scarcity of these holy things at their 'source', and no dearth of need for them in the world. The only lack lies in ourselves, in the human inability to call upon them adequately and channel them truly in our lives. The gates of heaven are never closed.

But all the same, we must be under no illusions that we can work miracles. We are only infinitesimal units in a vast arena of what is still unregenerate substance. We are but tiny points of energy in the sea of mankind. This recognition and acknowledgement is a necessary humility, an essential to keep our work true and clear and unclogged by glamour and false notions of what we can do.

Yet, at the same time it is important to realize that as dedicated individuals we can be a definite force for good. Each of us is a part of the current that will eventually become a spiritual tide. And we need never forget, when faced with the difficulties, disheartenments and disillusions that beset us inevitably from time to time, that we are literally the substance of that new tide and on our resilience its flow depends.

Another point it will profit us to remember is that not only have we the strength of comradeship on the outer planes with those, like-minded and co-dedicated, who are seeking to achieve the same ends, but on subjective levels our prayer, thought, invocation, brotherhood of spirit gather into an immense world power. We can have little idea, hemmed about as we are by the tribulations and divisions that harass mankind, of the Forces ranged on the side of Light and of the way that we, isolated—as we think— individuals can contribute to and receive from the amalgam of good on subtler planes.

Until we can verify these things for ourselves, we can only take assurance of them from those who are on ahead in their perceptions and penetrations into Truth. From them, from their example, teaching and affirmation we gather confidence that we are part of a great world force when we meditate and pray for mankind's benefit—for good to be made manifest. This confidence we need to give us the strength and positivity required for such work. In times of stress, world tension, conflict, tragedy, it helps to know that we are not alone, that on inner levels we belong to a 'society of Souls', a 'Company of Heaven', which is working unitedly and can have effect.

Many of us feel isolated in our daily lives from others treading the same path. But this is only another 'earth' illusion. As we become more conscious of our Souls, so our sense of unification with others also grows. A new awareness of our fellows on the path, a deep, quiet, inner certainty 'keeps us company' on the way. Here we have another of the divine paradoxes that form the stepping-stones along our path—our journey is often a lonely one, yet we have a thousand true, inner friends.

Finally, we should become aware that meditation is no five—or fifteen—minute process, but belongs to the twenty-four hours of the day. To begin with, we may harness ourselves slowly, yes, like gently bringing in a horse to work willingly in the shafts. But presently the inner life begins to assume more lasting proportions in our daily consciousness; it wraps itself around us, enveloping us in its quietitude and its strong arms.

Meditation then comes to be a daylong matter, an absorption into new areas that lasts in our consciousness throughout the day and sustains us through all outer activity. Slowly it eliminates the habits of the market place, the philosophy of the tangibles, the race to be free. Gradually it establishes the life force of the inner worlds and brings us the ultimate benediction of *knowing* that we and our Souls are one. The Persian poet Kahlil Gibran put it in this pictorial form:

> He to whom worshipping is a window,
>> to open but also to shut,
> has not yet visited the house of his soul
>> whose windows are from dawn to dawn.

There are no short cuts in the process and all parts of ourselves are involved. Our approach to divinity must be an affair of the heart as well as the mind. Our experiences have to work on us, fining us out, rendering us more sensitive, more able to respond. In Goethe's words:

> Who never spent the midnight hours
> Weeping and watching for the morrow,
> He knows you not, ye heavenly Powers.

And even then, when we have exercised all our endeavours, fulfilled all the requirements we have been taught are needed, the true knowing only slips across in the silence beyond the perimeter of self. Out on those frontiers we find the ultimate experience, come to know that we are God, not just in a mystical ecstasy, but through a divine insight that establishes for us this truth. These fruits of meditation can never be taken away from us, even though they may be temporarily forgotten. They are first hand knowledge that will last for all time.

Since we must always share our blessings, radiate our God-hood, perhaps the best ending to this study of meditation is the following formula which can be used to send out the gifts of the spirit to the world. It is based on the Buddhist 'Blessing of the Four Divine States', and through it we align ourselves with these divine qualities and then, using all our meditative powers, build a channel for each of them in turn and send them out to bless and redeem.

It is a method that is quite simple, but it may be used to meet any particular need in the world as well as generally and pervasively. It need take only a few minutes, yet if we do it each day, joining with the thousands working the same way, how much spiritual energy is being conducted into mankind's aura to lift and heal? This is one of the mysteries we cannot know yet, but it is also one of the inspiring thoughts that entice us onwards, stimulate our efforts and encourage us ceaselessly to try to walk as Souls.

Blessing of the Four Divine States

Having made a rapid alignment along the usual lines, visualize the earth as a globe bathed in light. Standing as a transmitter of the qualities invoked and endeavouring to send them especially to places of particular need, say, aloud if possible:

Love to all beings—
     North—South—East—West—Above—Below
Love to all beings.
     (Pause for a few moments of silent radiation.)

Compassion to all beings—
     North—South—East—West—Above—Below
Compassion to all beings.
     (Radiation)

Joy to all beings—
     North—South—East—West—Above—Below
Joy to all beings
     (Radiation)

Serenity to all beings—
     North—South—East—West—Above—Below
Serenity to all beings.
     (Radiation)

So let it be.

APOLOGIA

So many words has it taken to trace the Silent Path of Meditation—words, when silence is the true medium! Yet such is inevitably the complication of the way by which mankind proceeds on the long journey from the Infinite to the finite and back to Infinity again.

It is the dharma or task, destiny and at the same time privilege of the human kingdom above all others to interpret divinity, combine spirit and matter, express God-ship consciously in form. To mankind has fallen supremely the task of resolving the situation that St John described in his *Revelation*—'The light shineth in the darkness and the darkness comprehendeth it not.'

And so we are always faced with the problem of 'form'. It is our field of action and our means. It creates our difficulties, problems, obstructions, yet it is also our way of achieving, of both lifting and being lifted up.

We must utilize words, therefore, at least until that time when we can work with some degree of formlessness on subtler levels. But words must be kept in their place. There is constant danger of their misinterpretation for they have a living quality, creative yet chameleon-like and illusory, changing their meaning surreptitiously and conveying different things to different perceivers. This we should always be aware of, taking them only so far as they go, waiting within ourselves to find their truth and confirmation. Lin Yutang went so far as to say 'He who talks about the truth injures it.'

And the Chinese sage, Lao Tzu observed 'Many words lead to exhaustion', and it is more than time that these pages were ended. But it is to be hoped that they will be only the beginning for the reader who has borne with them all and that they will provide at least some rough design or framework, in the centre of which the true work will be done. As we read in the Tao Teh King:

You fashion clay to make a bowl,
   the usefulness of the bowl is always in that empty
   innermost.
You cut out doors and windows to make a house,
   their usefulness is always in their empty space.
Therefore profit comes from external form,
   but usefulness comes from the empty innermost.

So it will always be with all forms of meditation and all words that we use to frame our thoughts. This Apologia is therefore not addressed so much to the reader, who needs must get down to his own meditation, as to the Spirit of Silence, to whom we must pay our respects and into whose presence we must enter to achieve any measure of the reality of the higher way.

Silence is no passive thing. It is a vibrant presence which fills any vacuum in sound and conveys its own living quality. Most of us know the truth of the phrase 'the silence that sounds', and the old adage 'silence is golden' means more than just that it is safe or wise. It means that it is golden in the sense of being filled with light.

In its secret depths power is generated, problems are solved, realizations are reached, sensitivity is developed; in them we are recharged, regenerated, renewed. And silence carries healing on its wings. It may never press its case, but it needs to be given adequate recognition, for in meditation of any value it must fundamentally reign.

The value of silence has long been taught and although it has been especially revered in the East, its practice has been an almost universal requirement in all efforts to approach the inner worlds. The silent vigil has been demanded of the neophite in almost every faith and sphere. It invariably preceded his crowning moments or initiation, and the final words of the hierophant in the Mystery rites—'Go in Peace!'—meant inner stillness, silence in heart, mind and soul.

Yet today it is becoming a rare, if not unobtainable, gift. The man-made sounds being multiplied by our evolution are rapidly extending their tentacles over the globe like some strange giant or ever-expanding octopus. In the face of this, we have to make new penetrations into silence, go further into its holy temple to find our shrine. This can be done. We have always been taught of an inner as well as outer silence, even though it may be harder to find.

As well as ask its blessing, we must, however, serve silence too. 'Govern the lips as they were palace-doors, the King within', we read in *The Light of Asia*, where there is much of the Buddha's teaching on right discourse—the right balance between silence and speech. There are many aspects of silence, many ways to serve it and invoke it within and about ourselves, that we may stand as its sentinels, guarding the 'king within', standing steady in the midst of the noise that permeates the world.

This is, of course, the dual life required of all who seek to tread the Path; it is the holding of the inner and outer lives in balance, keeping the presence of silence in our hearts while fulfilling our commitments throughout the day. So we take our place in what Francis Thompson spoke of in his poem *The Kingdom of Heaven* as—

The traffic of Jacob's Ladder,
Pitched between heaven and Charing Cross.

No easy position—though at least not complicated by
traffic congestion like the Strand! This may seem to bring us
back to where we began, faced with the problems of fitting
in the meditative life. But we are a step or two further on.
We are better equipped, with more knowledge, more
prowess, more intention than if we had never examined the
ways and means of the Silent Path. Like the Prodigal Son,
we have explored and added to ourselves sufficient to *decide*
to make our return, and have also ascertained a little more
about the 'home-coming' we may expect.

Now the words are finished. The rest lies in the doing of
it and in the heart and head of each, alone. For when all is
said and done, it is only when something deep within us calls
out that we must explore this path, cries out for union with
the Higher Self so loudly that we have to pay attention, that
we really set ourselves to steady meditation and the disciplines of the inner path. Then we are willing to make the
needed forfeitures and come, cap in hand, with a kind of
joyous expectancy, a feeling that a 'hunch' of long ago is
coming true, and we are ready to explore the silence and use
for good the powers that we find.

'The gliding of the mind's boat into the lagoon of the
spirit is the gentlest thing I know,' wrote Paul Brunton. 'It
is more hushed than the fall of eventide.' If, in the midst of
our daily lives, we can still ourselves sufficiently to launch
our meditation in this way, we shall reach the secret places of
the Soul without fail.

So, let us call a halt and symbolically uncover our heads—
open ourselves—and stand alert, attuned, focussed. The
Tibetans have a saying 'Signs from the Soul come silently,
as silently as the sun enters the darkened world.' And we
must still ourselves and listen, so that we do not miss too much.

ACKNOWLEDGEMENTS

Acknowledgement is made to the following publishers and authors, whose permission to quote from the books mentioned is gratefully appreciated:

Rider and Co.: *The Secret Path* and *The Wisdom of the Overself* by Paul Brunton.

The Lucis Publishing Co.: *Letters on Occult Meditation, From Intellect to Intuition, The Light of the Soul, Discipleship in the New Age* and *The Externalisation of the Hierarchy*, all by Alice A. Bailey.

The Ananda Publishing House: *The Yoga of the Kathopanishad*, by Sri Krishna Prem.

A. P. Watt and Son and the executors of Sir James Frazer: *The Golden Bough*, by Sir James Frazer.

Psychosynthesis Research Foundation: *Psychosynthesis*, by Roberto Assagioli.

E. P. Dutton and Co. Inc.: *Cosmic Consciousness*, by Richard Maurice Bucke.

The Theosophical Publishing House, Adyar: *Concentration*, by Ernest Wood.

The Clarendon Press, Oxford: *Eastern Religions and Western Thought*, by S. Radhakrishnan.

Vincent Stuart and John M. Watkins Ltd: *The Yoga of the Bhagavat Gita*, by Sri Krishna Prem.

Collins Publishers: *Letters from a Traveller* and *Hymn of the Universe*, by Teilhard de Chardin.

Chatto and Windus Ltd and Mrs Laura Huxley: *The Perennial Philosophy*, by Aldous Huxley.

Macmillan and Co. Ltd: *Sadhana*, by Rabindranath Tagore.

Sri Aurobindo Ashram: A Poem by Sri Aurobindo.

Finally, and above all, I should like to express my great and lasting gratitude to D.K. for his inspiration, to R.A. for his interpretation and to N.M. for her unfailing and unlimited help on all levels.

M. J. E.

BIBLIOGRAPHY

of books referred to and quoted.

The Bhagavad Gita (Johnston translation) (Johnston, Flushing, New York).

Concentration by Ernest Wood (The Theosophical Publishing House, Adyar).

Cosmic Consciousness by Richard Maurice Bucke (Dutton and Co. Inc., New York).

The Dhammapada, translation by Narada Thera (John Murray).

Discipleship in the New Age by Alice A. Bailey (Lucis Publishing Co., New York).

The Externalisation of the Hierarchy by Alice A. Bailey (Lucis Publishing Co., New York).

Eastern Religions and Western Thought by S. Radhakrishnan (The Clarendon Press, Oxford).

The Golden Bough by Sir James Frazer (Macmillan and Co. Ltd).

Hymn of the Universe by Teilhard de Chardin (Collins).

From Intellect to Intuition by Alice A. Bailey (Lucis Publishing Co., New York).

Letters from a Traveller by Teilhard de Chardin (Collins).

Letters on Occult Meditation by Alice A. Bailey (Lucis Publishing Co., New York).

The Light of Asia by Sir Edwin Arnold (Kegan Paul).

The Light of the Soul by Alice A. Bailey (Lucis Publishing Co., New York).

Magic and Mystery in Tibet by Alexandra David-Neel (Souvenir Press, London).

On Vital Reserves by William James.

The Perennial Philosophy by Aldous Huxley (Chatto and Windus).

Psychosynthesis by Roberto Assagioli (Hobbs, Dorman and Co., New York).

The Secret Path by Paul Brunton (Rider and Co.).

Tao Teh King, translation by Isabella Mears (Theosophical Publishing House, London).

The Travel Diary of a Philosopher by Hermann Keyserling.

The Wisdom of the Overself by Paul Brunton (Rider and Co.).

The Yoga of the Bhagavat Gita by Sri Krishna Prem (John Watkins).

The Yoga of the Kathopanishad by Sri Krishna Prem (The Ananda Publishing House, Allahabad).

INDEX